# ADLAI STEVENSON

# ADLAI
# STEVENSON

By
JOHN BARTLOW MARTIN

New York
HARPER & BROTHERS *PUBLISHERS*

*To my wife, Fran*

# Contents

# ADLAI STEVENSON

# A Trip with Stevenson

In 1952, for the first time in modern American history, a genuine presidential draft occurred. The word draft is almost universally misunderstood. Politicians have used it so often to describe rigged nominations that most people have concluded that a genuine draft never occurs. By and large, this is true. But one did occur in 1952: The Democrats drafted Adlai Stevenson.

This draft occurred because Harry S. Truman's exit from the presidency created a tremendous vacuum. The void at the head of the ticket had to be filled. And more, for the first time in twenty years the conglomerate Democratic majority was obliged to rearrange itself around a new man. All spring the party tortuously explored the possibilities. Then for five July days at the Chicago stockyards it groped through issues and candidates. Finally it plucked from his secure obscurity Adlai E. Stevenson and thrust him before the great pitiless eyes of television, a rather small, slightly frail man with a too-big nose and kindly eyes and a manner that somehow suggests that of the schoolboy always trying to make sure his coat is buttoned, to remember to keep his shoulders back. And Stevenson, after months of soul-searching, accepted.

The draft must have puzzled a lot of people. Not often is a

presidential nomination repeatedly tendered and refused and finally thrust upon a man, as this one was on Stevenson. Why did he behave as he did? And why did the party put up with it? Watching the curious unreality of the springtime non-campaign, watching the heaving sea at the stockyards, people must have wondered, "What goes on here?"

What went on was extremely complex but it has a simple explanation. That explanation lies in the character of Adlai Stevenson. Stevenson's character—his mind, his background, his natural bent—explain both why the Democrats had to draft him and why he didn't want to run.

When Stevenson campaigned for Governor of Illinois in 1948, his friends used the slogan, "The New Look in Illinois Politics." The phrase had more meaning, it has turned out, than they realized.

Stevenson is a new kind of man in American politics. To understand him is to understand the strange presidential year of 1952.

What kind of man is he? What is his background, who are his friends, what does he look like? How does his mind work? How did he become Governor of Illinois, and what has he done as Governor? What are his views on national issues?

I went down to Springfield to try to answer some of those questions April 1. It happened that the Governor was scheduled to make a routine trip that day, visiting two state institutions and making an after-dinner talk at a small-town Rotary meeting, and I arranged to tag along, not to interview Stevenson but to observe him in action.

After lunch he came into the office of his appointment secretary on the ground floor of the Executive Mansion, ready to leave. He had his hat on, a brown hat with a very narrow brim, and he was holding a briefcase with one hand and thrusting his other hand upward into the sleeve of his topcoat. He was still talking to an assistant following him: "This thing of being neutral in local primaries reminds me of the fellow who said, 'It's all right to be neutral but who are we neutral against?' "

The Governor turned to leave but caught sight of Fred Hoehler, Director of the Department of Public Welfare and one of the men closest to him. Stevenson said, "I'll be visiting Rednour this afternoon—what's your present feeling about him?"

Hoehler said, "I think he's doing a good job."

The Governor nodded, said, "Good," and walked to the front door of the Mansion, followed by two of his sons, an administrative assistant named Larry Irvin, and me. A State Police Captain, Emmet Van Diver, stood beside the Governor's old black Cadillac, which was drawn up under the portico directly in front of this ground-floor door. The Governor got into the back seat. His younger son, Borden, sat beside him and I sat next to Borden.

As the others got into the front seat, the Governor's dog, a big black and white spotted coach dog, jumped onto the Governor's lap. Stevenson laughed and fended him off. A policeman moved to open the door and remove the dog but Stevenson said, "He's all right," and the car rolled down the breast of the knoll from the Mansion and headed smoothly past the towering State Capitol and through the Springfield traffic and, gathering speed, on out through the countryside toward the airport.

Stevenson's morning had been a harried one—the pressure upon him was increasing almost hourly, the pressure of telephone calls and visits by pilgrims to the Mansion that had suddenly, since three days earlier when President Truman had renounced renomination, become a power center in the 1952 presidential campaign. This was the first chance Stevenson had had in several days to get out of the Mansion and to spend some time with his boys. His time with them is severely limited. Adlai

III is a senior at Harvard, Borden a freshman. They were visiting him this week during their spring vacation but politics had interfered with their visit, as it does with everything else.

Stevenson got the dog quieted down and leaned back in his corner of the car, saying, "I feel like a kid on an outing from school. I do like to show the boys as much of the State as I can. Also, I'm about a year overdue on my visit to Menard and Chester." Menard is the State Penitentiary for southern Illinois. It is located at Chester, Illinois, and almost adjoining it is the Illinois Security Hospital. Bert Rednour, about whom the Governor inquired as he left the Mansion, is superintendent of the Hospital. Rednour, a former county chairman, is one of two politicians whom Stevenson appointed as superintendent of a Welfare Department institution; his other superintendents are nonpolitical.

The Governor went on chattily, "Have you ever been down to Menard Penitentiary? This is a terrible place. This is the sinkhole. It was established many years ago, in 1872, I think—when," he asked, raising his voice, "was Menard established anyway?" Nobody knew. "It was about 1872 anyway. It was established as a piece of political log-rolling at a time when southern Illinois had an importance that it has since lost. Importance population-wise, that is. Menard is really an appalling place. It's hotter than the hinges in the summer. It sits right down in a rock quarry. That's why they located it there—in those days they didn't know what to do with prisoners except work them on the rock pile. But now the quarry's about worked out so there the prison sits, at the bottom of an abandoned quarry. It's absurd. The prison farm is scattered all around, too, noncontiguous property, purchased, I suppose, as another piece of political log-rolling."

The dog, named King Arthur but called Art, was climbing

onto my lap and the Governor said, "Watch out—he'll scratch your briefcase. Scratched mine all up."

He went on, "They process tobacco for state institutions at Menard, you know, and we found we were paying an appalling price for the flavoring. It seems to have been some kind of a racket. And a very considerable amount of money was involved too, curiously enough. We finally got rid of that."

He gazed out the window at the flat Illinois countryside. His face was relaxed. He seemed to be enjoying himself. The day was bright and beautiful.

Suddenly he said, "Do you know about the so-called Chemco Project?" I said I didn't. Talk of Menard had brought to his mind the plight of the whole southern part of Illinois, called Little Egypt, a depressed area. Chemco is a $400,000,000 project to improve Little Egypt's economy. "We're trying to get inter-state financing on it. A friend of mine is working on it. Ferdinand Eberstadt." (Eberstadt is a New York investment banker influential in American affairs during the recent war.)

At the airport we got into a small plane, a twin-engined, four-passenger Beechcraft. The Governor's son Adlai sat in the co-pilot's seat up front beside the pilot. The plane taxied for the take-off and before it was in the air the Governor had excused himself—"I've got a little reading to do"—and settled back to read an article on his presidential prospects by Bernard DeVoto in *Harper's Magazine*.

Governor Stevenson is fifty-two years old. He is just under five feet ten inches tall. He weighs 190 pounds. He has put on fifteen pounds—"most of it around the middle," he says—since being elected Governor in 1948. In private life he exercised a lot, mostly tennis and horseback riding, but as Governor has lacked the time to do so. Governing is a sedentary occupation.

His face has aged considerably in the last four years too. It it deeply seamed. He has always had a high forehead; now it runs almost to the back of his head. What hair remains is black. His features are uneven. He has a big, irregularly shaped nose. His eyes are blue and very large and very round, almost banjo-eyes. His eyebrows are high and unruly, which tends to give him a skeptical expression. His skin is freckled and blemished with moles. It is rather dark, the kind that tans well. His is the sort of face that one notices in a group and catalogues as belonging to an "interesting" or "distinguished" man. It is an intelligent face.

On the day of our trip Stevenson was wearing a dark blue pin-striped suit. It was a little mussed. He wore an old brown hat and carried an old brown gabardine topcoat. He was wearing a white shirt made of Oxford cloth with a button-down collar. The collar was a trifle frayed.

He sat with his briefcase on his lap, holding his magazine almost at arm's length. He reads rather slowly and carefully. After a time he closed the magazine, put his glasses away, hauled his briefcase and coat and pants legs upward in one quick gesture, stretched his legs and crossed his ankles, and leaned back and closed his eyes. In a few minutes he was asleep. He cat-naps whenever he gets a chance.

The countryside below had been flat, a neat Midwest checkerboard, sunlight glinting on the roofs of evenly spaced barns and farmhouses, but now the country was getting hilly, the neat pattern was broken, and in the southwest distance appeared a narrow snaky ribbon, the Mississippi.

The plane began to descend through a cloud bank; in the half-darkness it bumped sharply and slewed. Stevenson stirred uneasily, settled deeper into his seat. He likes to fly "because it saves so much time." He flies some fifty thousand miles a year, mostly in Illinois. Often he works aloft—"You can't get much done in the office because of the telephone."

The pilot was pointing out Menard Penitentiary to young

Adlai. Irvin, a man of forty-one in a gray suit who handles downstate patronage for the Governor, sat up straight and looked out. It was the first time he had moved in the fifty-minute flight.

The air was very rough. Across the river the plane banked round the small airport, tilting steeply. Stevenson awoke. "Here we be," he said, and then, looking downward at the close ground sailing past, "You notice how green it is here with the winter wheat coming up?" He yawned. His hand was fumbling absently with the safety belt. The plane went down steeply for a landing but then rose, as though the pilot had changed his mind. Stevenson reached into his pocket and pulled out the letter inviting him to speak at Nashville tonight.

The plane hit. It bounced hard, upward and sideways, and it tilted hard to the left. The motors roared louder, the plane shuddered. Stevenson looked up, his eyes open wide with fright. He said, "What the hell?" The plane dropped again, bounced again. He said, "Did we blow a tire?" The plane was on the ground, running smoothly on the runway. Finally it stopped near the hangar.

Stevenson got up, opened the door, put out the ladder, clambered down, and the rest of us followed. Two or three men were walking toward us. Stevenson asked the pilot, "Did we blow a tire?"

"No, I'm sorry about that. It was the crosswind on the short runway."

The men meeting us had arrived and Stevenson turned and performed the introductions. Bert Rednour, superintendent at the Illinois Security Hospital, a stocky powerful man, began talking at once and almost never stopped during the Governor's visit. He said first, "Well, Governor, you did real good on television."

Stevenson laughed. "It was a rather rough experience."

Two days earlier Stevenson had appeared on a national network television program from Washington, "Meet the Press." The day before that, President Truman had declared to a Jefferson-Jackson Day dinner audience that he himself would not accept a presidential nomination. Stevenson on television had told his inquisitors that he would not make the same assertion but sought no other office than the governorship of Illinois. This week, during which Stevenson made the visit on which I accompanied him, he had suddenly become the leading candidate for the Democratic presidential nomination, though he had repeatedly disavowed such aspirations.

He got into the back seat of a small sedan beside Rednour, and I got into the front seat beside Browning Robinson, the warden at Menard Penitentiary, who drove. Stevenson's sons and Irvin rode in a State Police car that led the way. As we left the airport we passed a clump of bushes in yellow flower and Stevenson said, "Your season's so far ahead of ours at Springfield—look at that forsythia."

Rednour said, "It's been a wet spring so far," and talked about the weather as a farmer does. He mentioned that the peach trees were in blossom a little farther south near Anna this week. In Illinois, people tired of winter drive all the way from Chicago, some 360 miles, to view the peach trees near Anna. Stevenson said abruptly, "Are they? Damn me. Why didn't I think of that? I'd like to have shown that to the boys. They've never seen it. We could just as well have dropped down there." He looked at his watch. "But we've let the plane go now." Then, "How far is it to Nashville from here? We have to be there at six-thirty tonight."

"About fifty-five miles," said Rednour. There wouldn't be time to visit Anna.

Warden Robinson, a tall spare downstate man with a wide catfish mouth, said, as he drove along, "See those pits here,

Governor—that's where they filled the sandbags during the flood."

"*Is* it?" Stevenson said. "Well, well." Then, "Well, what's the news down here?"

Rednour said, "The news down here is you. Everybody wants you to run for Governor but they're scared to death you'll run for President."

Stevenson laughed, a deep abrupt chuckle. "I guess that's about the way I feel too."

Rednour said, "They feel it'd be an easy race against Taft but this Eisenhower, he's got a lot of popularity."

Stevenson asked, "What's the feeling down here about the military?"

"Well, I personally don't believe in a military man for President and I hear other people saying the same thing."

"Is that so?"

"Now that Taft, he'd be a walkaway for you," and he talked at length about a recent canvass of downstate county chairmen.

The car rolled across the Mississippi on a high spidery bridge, then turned off the main road and swung up the high bluff, climbing steeply. Rednour was saying they'd had an escape from the Security Hospital just the day before and he pointed out the route the runaway had taken across the bluff. Halfway up the hill the road was crumbling and Rednour began explaining the problem he was having with the road and the contiguous land—"There's an old woman owns it lives in California and—" He caught sight of a school bus parked in front of the Hospital. "You're going to get to see a bunch of school children, Governor. They're going through the institution today."

Stevenson said nothing. Like any other governor he sees a lot of school children. Getting out Stevenson gazed at the institution, its white paint dazzling in the spring sunshine. "It always looks spick-and-span here," he said.

Rednour said eagerly, "We painted it last fall," and took Stevenson's arm and guided him toward the door, saying, "Now, Governor, we want to show you through all we can here." The rest of us strung out behind.

### HOSPITAL FOR THE CRIMINAL INSANE

Inside, we left our coats and hats in Rednour's office, then started through the institution. Rednour introduced the Governor to every guard we encountered. At first he introduced the rest of us too. To save time I soon dropped back and so did Irvin and thenceforward Rednour simply introduced "the Governor and his two sons."

In the dining room we met the group of school children. They were eating cookies. Stevenson said, "Do we rate a cookie?" Rednour introduced him to the group and as we went on past, one of the kids said, "So that's Stevenson, huh?" and another, "That's him." Stevenson stepped alone into the kitchen and said "Hod-do," as he did many times that day. His inflection is a curious mixture of Midwest and Eastern speech. He was raised in an Illinois farm town and educated in the East.

He picked up a couple of cookies and munched them as we walked along. Coming upon a shirtless man sitting on a bucket cutting up potatoes, he asked how the potatoes were peeled. Rednour demonstrated a peeling machine. Stevenson kidded his boys about their prospects of doing kitchen police in the Army. The younger boy, Borden, who is nineteen, had visited his draft board that day. The elder, Adlai, is deferred until he finishes his school year at Harvard.

In the butchershop, Warden Robinson said, "This is where they make the Adlaiburgers." Everybody laughed, including Stevenson, though he did not seem greatly amused. Several months earlier he had been shocked to learn that state food inspectors apparently had connived with criminals to sell horse-meat for use in hamburger in Illinois; the Chicago *Tribune,* a Republican newspaper that opposes Stevenson, working hard at making political capital of the scandal, had invented the term "Adlaiburger."

In a ward Stevenson stopped in front of a row of empty cells and said, "Explain to us again about the four types of cases you have here," and gestured to his sons to come closer, saying, "I want you to hear this, boys." Rednour explained that the Security Hospital contained patients too violent to be kept at other state mental hospitals, persons accused of crimes but adjudged insane and therefore incapable of standing trial, convicts who had suffered mental breakdowns in penal institutions, and persons committed under the Illinois criminal sexual psychopath law. Rednour led the way up a winding narrow enclosed staircase, saying, "This next ward up here is the worst in the institution," then, thumping the walls of the staircase, "We painted this with our own labor."

Stevenson said, "But this stairway is still your only way out of the violent ward?"

"That's right."

"That's bad."

Upstairs in a big bare gray room pale sunlight slanted in through high windows, and about one hundred inmates were sitting around on benches. A few were playing checkers or cards. Most were just sitting, gray figures in their uniforms, against the wall. A half-dozen guards stood spaced out in front of them.

Our party walked slowly along the opposite wall. A few of the men looked up as the Governor passed. One called out, "If you run for President I hope you're elected." Another cursed him softly, mindlessly. A great hulking blond giant stepped out of the group and started forward. A guard reached for him.

He brushed the guard aside with a gesture and came on. Three guards escorting us stepped closer to the Governor nervously. Stevenson said, "This man wants to speak to me," and stopped and waited.

The Governor held out his hand. The man shook it. He said, "I want to speak to you, Governor. I don't belong in a mental institution. I'm a murderer. I'm not insane. I belong at Joliet. I'm not interested in beating a rap. All I ask is a chance to go to court and see if I was justified." (Prisoners in Illinois often use the word "justified" to mean "given justice.") Stevenson asked him some questions about his case. He answered rationally and firmly. Stevenson listened, cocking his head on one side and looking downward, a characteristic pose. He said, "I'll speak to Mr. Rednour and go over the records in your case." He walked on and in a moment said to Rednour, "You know his name, I suppose." Rednour did. As we left the ward, a man unseen on an upper tier of cells was screaming hoarse curses at the Governor, and an elderly guard near the door was looking upward and trembling with anger and muttering, "If you don't shut up, up there—" We went on out.

We visited the commissary, the intake room, the staff office, other wards. Stevenson walked very fast; I sometimes had to trot to keep up. As he left each place he visited, he, unlike the rest of us, invariably said to the people there, "Nice to see you," or "Glad to meet you." Decorum is bred so deep in him he could not shake it if he tried.

We stopped in front of a locked cell. A young man was sleeping in pajamas on a mattress on the concrete floor. His mouth was open and his face was red. Rednour said, "This is the runaway. Got away yesterday. He's a good boy, feeble-minded. They found him in Missouri. Darn if he didn't try to hang himself then."

"What's that?" Stevenson asked.

"Tried to hang himself."

"When?"

"He'll tell you. Open it up," he said to one of the guards, adding, "We'll have to watch him."

Stevenson, looking a trifle annoyed, said, "Has the doctor looked at him?"

"Oh, sure."

A guard volunteered, "I cut him down. I shook his head. His head wouldn't shake. In jail in Missouri, it was, where they caught him."

They opened the cell door. Rednour called to the lad, "John, John, wake up, John."

He did not stir.

A guard stepped into the cell and slapped his face gently, saying softly, "John. John. John, wake up, John, O John."

Stevenson, who was frowning, said, "Let him sleep," and turned to go.

The guard was still shaking the boy. Stevenson said, "Oh, let him sleep, he's obviously under morphine or something."

Rednour hesitated then, saying, "Originally he burnt some sheds down," walked on. The runaway had not stirred.

In another ward Rednour stopped in front of a cell and said, "Here's the only man here we have to keep in a cell twenty-four hours."

The man, a lean muscular Negro, displayed a legal-looking document. He held it so that the officials could read it but could not snatch it from him. His expression was harshly suspicious. Rednour said, "That's his discharge papers." Stevenson put on his glasses, glanced at the document, then put his glasses away. The man said, "I oughtn't to be here, Governor. I ought to be out."

"The court sent you here."

"They ought to let me out, not keep me locked up all the time."

"Well, you behave yourself and maybe they will."

He walked on. From among a group of inmates in a corner of the ward a voice called out, and Rednour led the way toward it. The youth that had called was blind. Rednour said, "What is it, blind boy?"

He wanted his radio back. They had taken it away from him because he had broken it. The group discussed the question briefly. Stevenson waited patiently. Off to one side stood a man in the strange frozen attitude of a cataleptic trance. The room was clean but it looked gray.

The party of visitors moved on. They stopped soon and Rednour and Stevenson began talking to a young inmate doing clerical work. He was a small thin man, possibly forty years old, with a pointed face, wearing steel-rimmed glasses. He rose immediately when the visitors approached. He held himself rigidly erect as he described with some pride the jobs he had held "on the outside." He mentioned his former address in Chicago and Stevenson said, "Oh, yes, down on the South Side in the Fifth Ward." The man described his work here in a precise almost prissy voice. He talked about his grown children. Rednour said, "Governor, this is a pitiful case. He never committed a crime in his life till he killed his own mother. And he don't know why he did it."

The man had begun to shake violently. His whole body shook. Stevenson pretended not to notice. The man reached into a desk and seized a large flat parcel wrapped in newspaper and began tearing the wrapping away, his hands shaking so he could hardly do it, his voice quavering as he explained that he had here some pictures of his son and his daughter and his daughter's wedding. (A huge inmate a little distance away was saying loudly, "I want to see the Governor," but a guard was shoving him back.) The little man was telling the Governor about the plans and accomplishments of his children, and Stevenson said several times, "Is that so?" and "I'm delighted," as though greatly interested. Stevenson was listening with obvious sympathy.

Finally he walked on, moving more slowly, as though thinking of something. Then his pace quickened again and once more he passed from room to room, peering at the inmates, shaking hands with the guards, laughing when a guard called, "We're all for you, Governor," and when an inmate called, "I hope you're the next President." Before leaving he talked to Rednour about politics and about the case of the big man who claimed he was wrongly incarcerated here. At the outside door Stevenson and his sons had to pose for an institution employee who wanted to photograph them with Rednour.

Walking to Warden Robinson's car he stopped and gestured out over the bluff and said, "Isn't that a beautiful view?" The sunlight was bright and hard on the Mississippi. Trees were budding on the hillside, a fruit tree was in blossom, the grass was turning green, a breeze came soft across the prairie, the sky was blue.

### MENARD PENITENTIARY

Warden Robinson drove him down the hill to Menard Penitentiary, which Robinson has in charge, an ancient institution with yellow stone walls built in a quarry on the face of the bluff. Entering, Stevenson motioned his sons closer and pointing to a date carved in stone, said, "Boys, this was built in 1876," and inside the cool administration building he said, "See those high ceilings." A group of officials was waiting, tall downstate men with Southern accents, one saying softly, "Governor, I'm glad to see you, sir."

The tour of Menard was rapid. Irvin kept glancing at his watch. Stevenson, seeing this, said nothing but walked fast and asked questions fast. Robinson talked less than Rednour. Stevenson asked more questions than he had at Chester. He asked about the rock quarry, asked whether every inmate had a set of radio earphones in his cell, asked whether four-twenty was not too early to serve the inmates their evening meal, asked whether Robinson was having trouble hiring guards (as most prison wardens are these days), asked about plans for a new building inside the wall.

As before, he said, "Hod-do" in a cheery voice to guards and convicts. His manner on such occasions is always cheery and buoyant yet somehow it doesn't seem cocky. He walked through the cindered dusty railroad yard to stand and gaze at the old quarry, shaking his head sadly, apparently at the thought of the institution's improvident location, its age and almost medieval aspect, and the hopelessness, within limits of the budget, of doing anything about it. A guard with a rifle in his hands looked down from a high round tower.

Stevenson led the way through the prison's shops, explaining them to his sons, and jokingly offering them a chew of the tobacco being cured. The younger son, Borden, who was wearing a checkered sport jacket and gray flannel slacks, stayed close to his father. Adlai III tended to hang back to ask questions of the guards. They had not been here before. Borden remarked that the place depressed him.

Two of the guards and the boys dropped back from the others and I joined them and we made a side trip to view the electric chair. It was located in a small building that also was used for other purposes. Fifteen or twenty convicts standing around in front of it fell silent and stepped back a pace or two as we approached, in the manner of extras in a movie crowd scene. Inside, other convicts did the same. The guards discovered they lacked the keys to open the door to the chamber containing the electric chair. In their zeal to please, the guards all went to get the keys, leaving the boys and another civilian and me alone with the convicts.

It occurred to me that this wasn't safe—in a Michigan prison awhile back convicts had seized Governor G. Mennen Williams as a hostage in an attempt to escape, and the thought of that incident had crossed my mind several times today. Apparently it didn't occur to anybody else. The guards returned and we viewed the chair, one of the guards saying to the two young Stevensons, "There's a boy named Chapman supposed to sit in that but your daddy gave him a stay of execution to get a new trial." Governor Stevenson has said he is opposed to capital punishment. Once when asked to grant executive clemency to a condemned man he said, "Although I do not personally believe in capital punishment, it is permitted by the law of Illinois and I find nothing to justify interference with the penalty imposed by the court."

As we walked back to the administration building, the prison band was playing in the yard, and long lines of convicts were marching in and out of the dining room, and Stevenson stood a long time, watching.

A prison official accompanying us broke the mood by remarking to Stevenson, "Lotta votes there—maybe you ought to let them all out."

Stevenson laughed, amused. "Trouble is, if you let them out you'd have no way of making sure they'd vote the right way."

He was in good spirits as he entered the warden's living quarters. These comprise an extraordinarily spacious and handsome apartment, a fact that Stevenson called jokingly to Warden Robinson's attention. He recalled a night he had spent here a year or so ago. Robinson pointed to a bedroom and said, "That's your room, Governor."

Stevenson said, "I'd like to lie down there now and sleep about a week."

He stepped out onto a second-floor porch overlooking the Mississippi. "Here," he said, "is the best place of all. Sit up here on the porch in the evening, see the boats go by, hear the night sounds, smell the clover. It's wonderful."

The warden's wife offered them Cokes. Stevenson said he'd be delighted. (Irvin glanced uneasily at his watch.) Stevenson sat in the kitchen with Mr. and Mrs. Robinson, drinking his Coke from a bottle. He was breathing a little rapidly, probably because he had taken the steps to the warden's apartment two at a time. He looked tired and grateful for the opportunity to rest.

On the kitchen table was a copy of today's St. Louis *Post-Dispatch* with the headline:

DEMOCRATIC SCRAMBLE BEGINS AFTER TRUMAN BOWS
OUT OF RACE; STEVENSON STILL WON'T SAY YES.

Stevenson read the headline without comment. He turned abruptly to the warden's wife and said, "Well, Mrs. Robinson, how's your husband behaving himself?"

She laughed and made some reply. She was a plain, pleasant-faced woman. She said, "We wish you could visit us more often."

He nodded. "I know. I do too."

"I know it's hard to find time."

He shook his head. "It's just damn—" sucking in his breath so as to make the expletive almost inaudible "—near impossible. There just isn't any time. I just yesterday got around to going to Manteno," a state hospital for the insane. He had stopped there on his way back from the momentous week end in Washington. "And they're doing something at Manteno I'm terribly interested in too—this ultrasonic method of brain operations." He told them more about it. Their attention wandered a bit.

They asked where he was going tonight. To a Rotary meeting, he said.

"That reminds me," Warden Robinson said, "I'm going to talk to Kiwanis myself next week—what can I say for you?"

"You can say," Stevenson said, his eyes twinkling, "that he's been a mighty fine governor and we ought to keep him here."

Mrs. Robinson said, "We're afraid all these nice things they're saying about you, you'll run for President."

Stevenson said, "Isn't it terrible?"

"Well, no," she persisted. "I think it must be very gratifying. But we all hope you'll stay in Illinois."

"As if I haven't got enough trouble here without biting off some more," Stevenson said, then sighed, leaned forward, sat poised a brief moment, then set his Coke bottle decisively on the table and got up and said good-by and hurried downstairs.

He started to leave the institution, changed his mind, once more went through the two locked gates, visited small rooms where two members of his Parole Board were holding hearings on prisoners' cases, and finally left. Irvin said softly, "I think we'll make it this time," and glanced at his watch—5:30 P.M., with fifty-five miles to go to Nashville for a 6:30 arrival.

### A DRIVE IN THE COUNTRY

The road to Nashville ran over gullied country, redbud ablaze on the hillsides, sycamores white in the creek bottoms, tumble-down hovels scattered along the ridges, and once we passed an old unused covered bridge over Marys River, the first toll bridge in Illinois, said the State Policeman driving. Starting out for Nashville I rode with Irvin in the police car so that Governor Stevenson could be with his sons in the other car. Before long, however, the car in which they were riding had a flat tire. They got in with us and we drove on.

Stevenson, settling himself in his seat, said, "The last time

I had a flat tire was with that big Cadillac in Chicago. I was late for a speech and I got out and walked two or three blocks and found a police car and told the policeman, 'I'm Governor Stevenson—can you give me a ride to the Loop so I won't be late for a speech?' The one policeman turned to the other and said, 'I thought I'd heard 'em all but I never heard that one before.' "

The car rocked along pleasantly. The sun was setting. Stevenson said, "Isn't it a beautiful evening?" He looked out at the darkening hills, flattening now into a plain. He said to the State Trooper, "How were your quail down here last fall?"

"Pretty good, sir."

"I was out once near Vandalia. Didn't have much luck. Did better right near Springfield." We talked about shooting and shotguns. The Governor said he enjoyed hunting and had done a good deal of it in South Carolina. "A friend of mine has a plantation there. But," he said, "I don't get much chance to do that sort of thing in this business." He pointed at a tower off in a field. "What's that—a fire tower? That's one of ours, isn't it?"

"Yes, sir," the young trooper said.

"I suppose they're only manned in the dry season."

We passed a truck carrying some livestock. "Goats," Stevenson said. "Did you see them, boys? You hardly ever see them any more."

Borden asked how far south of Chicago we had been at Menard. Stevenson was able to tell him almost exactly, locating Menard in relation to Chicago, Springfield, and St. Louis, and urging Borden to check on a map.

A woman driving alone passed us. Stevenson leaned over to see our speedometer. Seventy miles an hour.

"What's she doing, Officer? Eighty-five?"

"Oh, maybe seventy-five, seventy-eight," he said, smiling.

Stevenson said, "This is a nice piece of road here." Rehabilitating Illinois' decrepit roads has been one of Stevenson's major projects, as we shall see.

We passed a deserted farmhouse and Stevenson pointed it out to the boys, remarking, "There's a farmer couldn't make it." He discoursed on the quality of the land hereabouts in a knowledgeable way.

As we drove along, Stevenson kept remarking about things he saw, calling things to the boys' attention, asking questions. His waking mind is never at rest. He has an inquisitive mind. He verbalizes a good deal too. Once he said to the policeman, "I want to see that grave of Shadrach Bond," and inasmuch as we were close to a cemetery at the moment the policeman put on the brakes, but Stevenson said, "No—Bond's grave is back at Chester. I just wondered if it's easy to find." The policeman thought a moment, then identified Bond. He said the grave was well marked. I asked who Bond was. "The first Governor of Illinois," Stevenson said, "1818 to 1822. I've never visited his grave. The old capital was at Kaskaskia, you know. What were the circumstances of his death, do you know, Officer? Did he die on the island?" The policeman didn't know. Neither did any of the rest of us. Stevenson's knowledge of Illinois history crops out constantly.

It was almost dark. Irvin was looking at his watch. He asked if tonight's speech was to be made before the Rotary Club of Nashville. Stevenson said, "It's two Rotary Clubs combined for the occasion, I believe—Nashville and Carlyle." He chuckled. "The Nashville Rotary has twenty-three members, I understand. This is an engagement I made some time ago and only because the man from the Nashville Rotary writes such an absolutely enchanting letter. He's been writing to me a couple of years, asking me to come down. He writes an exquisite letter —witty, clever, charming."

The policeman suggested that this was April Fools' Day. Stevenson said, "I completely forgot. Maybe there won't be any meeting or anything at all."

The car slowed and drove into Nashville, a town of 2,500, dark now. The streets near the old courthouse were quiet. Stevenson said, "It's the Lutheran Church, isn't it? I haven't any idea where it is. Pull in here and we'll find out," and the policeman swung into a filling station and Stevenson rolled his window down and said to two young boys putting air into a bicycle tire, "Boys, where's the Lutheran Church?"

They looked up, puzzled, then one of them recognized him and turned pale and began to stammer, "The church? Lutheran Church?"

Irvin said, "Where's the meeting?"

"Oh," the boy said, "you mean the Evangelical Parish Hall," and turned and pointed. "Two blocks down and two blocks over."

Stevenson said, "Thank you," and as we drove on he chuckled. "I guess I got the wrong denomination."

The street was bumpy. Cars were parked on both sides and a crowd filled the sidewalk. We stopped in the middle of the street, there being no other place to stop, and Stevenson said, "We're right on the beam—six-thirty." The young policeman said diffidently, "I want to thank you, sir, for what you've done for us," meaning that Stevenson had taken the State Police out of politics. Stevenson said, "You're doing a good job," then, handing his briefcase to Irvin and saying, "I guess I'll let you be custodian of the documents," he got out of the car and walked briskly across the sidewalk and walked alone undefended into the waiting crowd, which swallowed him greedily.

### WITH THE ROTARIANS

The rest of us followed. Irvin disappeared into the basement room where the dinner was to be served. I fell to talking to a voluble local Rotarian. "You're from Chicago, you say? You don't look like a city slicker. You don't look much different from us. You know, it used to be you could tell the farmers on the street but now they look just like anybody else." He described the advantages of small-town life. He told me about the crops hereabouts and about the coal mining. (In this county the Centralia mine blew up in 1947, killing 111 men, and a political scandal that ensued helped elect Stevenson Governor.)

Everybody seemed to be going upstairs so we went too. The crowd, some two hundred men and women, was packed into a varnished room and a white-haired man was pushing Stevenson and his sons against a wall and then the people began filing past, shaking hands with them. The boys looked boyish and a little ill at ease, Borden dropping one shoulder deprecatingly as the citizens shook his hand and uttered pleasantries. Some of the women being introduced were smartly dressed, some of the men looked like city executives; most were red-necked men in hard worsted suits and gaudy neckties, women in flowered print dresses, and, acknowledging their introductions, the men bobbed their heads and looked at the floor, the women looked away.

The press of the crowd was great, the room was very hot, but everyone seemed good-natured. One man leaving said jokingly, "Put your hands on your pocketbooks," and another, "We better go downstairs—the beans is on," and the toastmaster, Dr. Fred W. Schroeder, a tall bespectacled man, said fretfully, "I'm afraid if he shakes hands with all those people the dinner'll get cold." A woman leaving said, "Well, he sure has two nice-looking boys." Another said, "Now when he's President we can say we shook hands with him," and her husband, "If and when."

Matters moved expeditiously: the reception took about fifteen

minutes. Then all went down to the basement hall, a long room
in which stood five long tables set for dinner, folding slat-backed
chairs in place. The room was bare, steam pipes running along
the low ceiling. Governor Stevenson went to the speakers' table
and I found a place at another table with his two sons and
Irvin. Dr. Schroeder, the toastmaster, tapped his water glass
smartly and called several times, "Come to order, please," then,
"All face the flag to the southeast," then, when we had done
so, "Sing one verse of 'America.'" We did, accompanied by a
piano near the flag. A clergyman delivered a long invocation
and we sat.

Irvin, folding his napkin, pointed to the speakers' table.
In front of Stevenson's place was a lectern. Irvin said, "Ten
Bibles. I had to get ten Bibles to prop it up so it'd be high
enough." I had wondered what he'd been doing.

The toastmaster made a few brief remarks, saying that he
hoped to "make everyone feel that the Nashville Club is the
most friendly club in District 216," then presented the Nashville
Rotary president, Gordon Purdy, the man who had written
the letter that persuaded Stevenson to come here. He welcomed
the guests and members briefly, addressing Stevenson as "Your
Excellency," and saying he hoped this would be only the beginning of better relations between the Carlyle and Nashville clubs
and ending, "We extend to you not the keys to the city but
the hand of friendship. We, the Rotary Club of Nashville,
salute you, our neighbors. May this be a meeting you will long
enjoy."

Women, presumably the wives of Rotarians, began bringing
in large dishes of turkey, dressing, cranberries, mashed potatoes,
country gravy, green beans, corn, and rolls. Irvin said to me,
"One time last summer we made a swing through southern
Illinois and we had seven fried chicken dinners in a row. When

we got back to the Mansion, the Governor said, 'How'd you like to come in and have a cold chicken sandwich?' "

I asked Irvin if he thought Stevenson enjoyed this sort of thing. "I think he must," he said. "He likes to meet people and likes to speak. There are only 204 people here tonight—compared to 6,000 in Washington last Saturday." (He was referring to the Jefferson-Jackson Day dinner at which Truman had withdrawn from the presidential campaign.) "If the Governor didn't enjoy it he wouldn't come to a place like this. I mean, there aren't enough votes here to come for that reason. I think he enjoys it and I know he likes to tell people about government. That's what he's talking on tonight."

I asked Borden if he himself enjoyed it. He said he did, except that his right hand hurt from being shaken so much. I asked if he thought he'd enjoy the White House. He said, "I'm not thinking that far ahead." His father has said he'd cross that bridge when he came to it. A lanky man from a near-by town sitting across the table introduced himself, pointing to a card pinned to his lapel, and told the boys, "Our Rotary Club meets at six o'clock every Wednesday night and if you're ever down we'd like to have you as our guests."

Borden said, "Thank you very much."

I suggested to Irvin that the Governor had put in a long day, working in his office from 8:00 A.M. till 2:00 P.M., then starting on this trip. Irvin said, "This day is mild compared to some."

The diners finished at eight-fifteen and the women removed the dishes. Dr. Schroeder arose, tall, solemn, hawk-nosed. He suggested that people who wanted to turn their chairs around should do so now. A great scraping ensued. The floor was concrete. When the noise subsided Dr. Schroeder said, "We're very glad to have you here. There are too many of us and our program is too long to call on individuals so I will call on the various clubs and will they please stand. I shall try not to miss any. First, the flowers on the piano were presented by the Lions Club. I have two telegrams to read," and he read them. They congratulated the Nashville Rotary Club on this, its twenty-fifth anniversary. (The anniversary actually fell earlier; this celebration had been arranged to fit into Stevenson's schedule.) Schroeder read off the names of near-by towns and at mention of each the men and women representing them arose, in groups of anywhere from five to twenty—Centralia, Chester, Mt. Vernon, O'Fallon, Pinckneyville, Sparta (cheering at this name), Edwardsville, Benton, Marion, Staunton—coal towns and farm towns of southern Illinois. Applause greeted each. Schroeder asked if he had forgotten any, and voices called out "Vandalia" and "Du Quoin." Then the host clubs, Carlyle and Nashville.

Next a man named, according to the program, "Lloyd 'Davey' Sharp" stood beside the piano and, alone, sang a song. Schroeder then introduced Purdy, a youngish man who arose and introduced Stevenson. Purdy said, "Your speaker of the evening is here because of a challenge. When the twenty-fifth anniversary celebration was being planned, someone challenged me to write the Governor of Illinois and invite him, little thinking I'd do it. When challenged I'll do anything once." The audience laughed. "After the letter of acceptance came from Springfield, I shook and worried. Then I thought that this being Washington County and I being a Republican I'd be entirely among friends. The speaker is one of the enemy. It is he who must worry this evening—not I."

Stevenson half-rose, red-faced, and said hoarsely and loudly, "And he is." Stevenson was enjoying this.

Amid laughter, Purdy went on: "Until his office called and said one or two of his sons would be along, I was sure he would be the only Democrat in the crowd." He said he could add nothing to what was known about Stevenson, then introduced

him proudly as "the present and next Governor of Illinois."
Immediately Irvin was on his feet applauding, and all arose
and applauded.

When they were seated again, Stevenson, who was unopposed
this year in the Democratic primary for Governor, arose and
said, "I've seldom enjoyed an introduction more than that one
—but there is a possibility that you have frozen out all the
campaign contributions that I was looking forward to seeing."

He was tilting backward and forward slightly on the balls of
his feet. He was taking his glasses off and putting them on
again, as he does when nervous. "I was going to address you all
as fellow Democrats. The unhappy fact is that I can't even vouch
for my sons." Laughter. He had them coming his way. "I have
two reasons for being here. I haven't been here for a long while
and wanted to help celebrate your twenty-fifth anniversary—
and I delayed this trip because I enjoyed corresponding with
Mr. Purdy so much that I prolonged our correspondence as long
as I could. I met him for the first time this evening. And I am
going to give him a job. I'm going to make him poet laureate
of letter-writers of the State of Illinois."

The audience was with him now. He seemed to know it. His
nervousness vanished. His voice lost an edge of strain it had
had when he began. He said, "I've had a discussion with Dr.
Schroeder about how long I should speak. It is now twenty-three
minutes of nine," glancing at his wrist watch. "He suggested I
speak as long as I could keep the crowd interested. But that
would only be ten minutes, I told him. He said I should keep
going until such time as somebody fainted. It's all very perplex-
ing." He cut short the laughter: "It reminds me of a story about
a gentleman who addressed a large dinner party much, much
too long. When he finally finished the toastmaster arose and
said, 'Samson slew a thousand in a night with the jawbone
of an ass. Our guest speaker has just put *two* thousand to sleep

with the same implement and in only half the time.' " This time he waited for the laughter to cease.

He said, "My next perplexity was what to talk about tonight. But that's an absurdity—I always talk about the same thing. And that's your state government." He came down hard on the last sentence. It is indeed a dominant theme of his. "Tonight I'm going to talk about how we make both ends meet. Fiscal affairs and our budget." Once more, just as he seemed about to take up the manuscript visible on his lectern, he made another joke, as always when speaking on a subject difficult to make interesting: "I had no time to prepare properly for this speech, having been down in Washington warding off the countless thousands who want me to be president of the world." They laughed and called to him. He said, "When I first got into politics three years ago I went to a governors' meeting and one of the other governors said to me, 'You know, Mr. Stevenson, you've got quite a future if you'll just be careful. Always be careful of what you say. And what you do. Why, recently I was trying to pull up a window in the Executive Mansion and strained my back, and when it came out in the newspapers the story was that I had strained my back lifting a widow into the Executive Mansion.' "

That stopped the show. Waiting for the applause to subside, Stevenson glanced covertly at his watch. Five minutes had passed. He put on his glasses and addressed himself to his manuscript, glancing up to say, "So hang onto your hats and we'll talk about the budget of the State of Illinois. You as businessmen have to worry about your own budgets. My problem is making up a budget for a two-year period of something over $700,000,000—and then getting it through the Republican Legislature."

His voice is crisp and clear, clipped and exact. He is an expert speaker. He gets through long complicated sentences without faltering. In discussing the budget he was on familiar ground. Tonight's speech was a pasteup from two speeches he'd given recently. He made his main points forcefully—such as that he had managed during his tenure in office to keep the State's budget "in precarious balance." Constantly he put questions such as, "I wonder how many of you realize that you as taxpayers have to feed, clothe and shelter 48,000 welfare patients in addition to eight or nine thousand prisoners?"

Once Stevenson interpolated, "And, if I may advert to politics for a moment, I would like to stay in Illinois and see what I can do toward furthering these programs. I can only do it with the help and understanding of people like yourselves. This is a political year. I hope very much that we will not allow these sideshows to obscure the growing understanding of our larger interests." He went on. "Your interest is the public interest and so is mine. We are all on the same team—even if we don't all belong to the same party. What is good for business is good for government and vice versa."

He glanced at his watch. It was nine-five. He stopped speaking, put on his glasses, riffled the pages of his manuscript. He said, "This speech is so deadly I'm about to throw it all away." He shuffled the pages some more. "But there are some things that I should like to say, and though they are probably dull to you, I feel they are terribly important. Public servants who violate the public trust should be punished, severely, promptly. One dishonest public official is one too many. And so is one dishonest businessman." He raised a few national issues: control of inflation, protection of social security, revolution in the underprivileged areas of the world. Somewhere a telephone was ringing unanswered, and from the kitchen came a clatter of dishes.

He said, "It seems to me, Mr. Chairman, that I have long since exceeded the limits you set me." He laid his manuscript aside. "I am reminded of the little girl who told the minister after church, 'Mr. Minister, I liked your music but I thought your commercial entirely too long.'"

He sat down. All stood and applauded. Schroeder arose and said, "Why, you could have heard a pin drop except for an occasional cough. And if you care to be President of the United States I think you've made a number of votes." The crowd applauded loudly. Amid the noise Stevenson half-rose and called, "Can you say the same about being Governor of Illinois?"

After Schroeder, Purdy, and the president of the Carlyle Club had spoken a little more, and after the charter members had been introduced, and after Stevenson's sons and Irvin had been introduced, the meeting adjourned. The guests crowded around Stevenson to pick up copies of a state report he offered—"My goodness, I feel like a medicine salesman"—and seek his autograph. As soon as he gracefully could, he went out to his car. The rest of us followed and we drove away. It was nine-forty-five.

### GOING HOME

The Governor sat in the back seat with his boys. Borden said, "Good speech, Dad." Stevenson said something depreciatory. He seemed still stimulated by his performance. He asked Irvin, whom he often kids about being a politician, "Did we make any votes, Larry? Did you case the joint?" Irvin laughed. I remarked that Stevenson had jettisoned parts of his text. He replied, "My text is so wonderfully vapid that I can throw out three pages and never miss it."

He settled far back in the back seat, hidden by shadows. The car was the big seven-passenger Cadillac sedan; Captain Van Diver had driven it down here from Springfield during the afternoon. It was bought by the State in 1939. When two of

Stevenson's cabinet members recently urged him to get a new car, he said impatiently, "There's nothing wrong with the car I've got, let's talk about something else."

His son Adlai III asked if he had a radio over which we might hear some returns from the day's primary elections in Wisconsin and Nebraska. Captain Van Diver, driving, snapped the radio on and Irvin tuned it. He found the voice of Senator Estes Kefauver speaking on foreign policy. We were driving exactly seventy miles per hour. The lights were bright on the concrete. Captain Van Diver looked big and capable at the wheel. The radio program seemed to be a recorded symposium of the foreign policy views of leading candidates for the Democratic presidential nomination. Senator Robert S. Kerr followed Kefauver, then came Senator Richard B. Russell. Stevenson said, "Let's hear Dick Russell." Russell, it has transpired in recent months, is a cousin of Stevenson's. So is Vice-President Alben W. Barkley.

Russell finished and a new announcer, after a commercial, began broadcasting election returns, the old familiar phrases like "Incomplete returns from 645 precincts give—." Senator Robert A. Taft was leading in the Wisconsin presidential primary but with less votes than the combined totals of Governor Earl Warren and Harold E. Stassen. Stevenson murmured, "That knocks Taft out." (At the time it seemed so—after the big Minnesota write-in for General Dwight D. Eisenhower the week before, political soothsayers had been saying that if Taft polled fewer than a clear majority in Wisconsin his candidacy would collapse.) In Nebraska Taft was ahead, Kefauver was leading Kerr. We all listened rather attentively. The newscast ended, some music came on.

Stevenson fell to talking to his sons. His voice was too low to be clearly audible in the front seat but I got the impression they were talking family and personal matters—about the boys going into the armed forces, about young friends of theirs, Stevenson saying, "Say, your friend did himself proud," and "Will he go into the service now?" and once laughing deeply and relaxedly as though really enjoying himself. The boys divide their vacations from school between their parents, who are divorced. Stevenson spends as much time as possible with them during his share of their visit; their visit is one of the few occasions on which he appears to resent the demands of public life.

The Illinois plain was dark. We came to a town and Stevenson asked, "What's this?" "Greenville," said Captain Van Diver. The streets were dark and deserted. We passed the courthouse and Stevenson said to the boys, "That's one of those old courthouses they've taken the cupola off of."

"Why?" asked Borden.

"Just rehabilitating the buildings. Most of them have been condemned years ago."

Stevenson went back to talking to the boys. He was telling them what his schedule would be over the week end. He was to fly to Chicago Friday to address a political rally at lunch. Appointments in his Chicago office that afternoon. Saturday morning he would go to Quincy, 310 miles southwest, to dedicate a courthouse, then back to Rockford to meet the Prime Minister of Sweden. Sunday he had to make three speeches and put on his monthly television program on state government, plus luncheon and dinner engagements. Five speeches in all that week end, plus "a curtsy I've got to make at———" plus appointments. A heavy schedule, and the boys were due back in school Monday. Adlai III said, "I'd like to be with you when you see Arvey," that is, Colonel Jacob M. Arvey, boss of the Cook County Democratic machine. "Is that all right?"

"Sure."

"What's on between now and Friday?"

"Office work," that is, affairs of state, appointments with politicians, and, owing to the presidential boom, appointments with a dozen newspaper and magazine writers. "You can sit in on all those talks that you want to." And then: "What do you think John Fell will want to do this summer?" John Fell Stevenson is sixteen, the Governor's youngest son, a student at Milton Academy. "Does he want to go to Canada again?" They have many times visited in the Canadian summer home of a friend.

Borden said, "John Fell wants to go there every year."

Stevenson said, "I know. He doesn't seem to want to go back to that ranch."

Adlai started a discussion of somebody's views on politics, saying, "She's Jeffersonian, really. Largely on an abstract level."

We came to Highway 66, the main road running from Chicago to Springfield to St. Louis, and Stevenson informed the boys, "Now you're on 66." Traffic was heavy, mostly overland trucks, and we swung in and out among them, traveling fast, Captain Van Diver throwing his spotlight expertly on and off the truckers' rear-view mirrors before passing.

A radio announcer was saying, "Thirty-nine precincts in Nebraska out of two thousand give. . ." Then another voice came on, Eisenhower's. He was radioing a long report on the first year of NATO. Irvin and I listened. Stevenson was engrossed in talk with the boys. Toward the end of the speech Stevenson said rather sharply, "Who's that?"

Irvin said, "Eisenhower."

Stevenson said, in a voice that sounded almost awed, "I never heard him speak before," and we all listened till he had finished. Stevenson made no comment.

We reached Springfield, the houses along the outlying streets dark, and drove to the Executive Mansion behind the Abraham Lincoln Hotel and as we turned into the driveway that curves

up the gentle knoll Stevenson stretched and said, "Home again,"
then, "The light's still on in the library."

Inside, we went into the ground-floor office of Bill Blair,
Stevenson's appointment secretary, from which we had departed
that afternoon. Blair, a tall urbane man of thirty-five in gray
flannel and buttoned-down collar, was sitting at his desk listening to election returns on the radio. He handed Stevenson a
*Collier's* containing a picture layout on Senator Kefauver.
Pointing to a photograph of Kefauver's young children in a
bathtub, Blair said, "They want to do one on you next week,
they want to get Borden and Adlai and John Fell and you all
in a bathtub, think that can be arranged?" Stevenson laughed.
He looked tired. He sat down on a sofa, saying, "I'll be ready
for some sleep." He got up and went into the bathroom. Blair
turned the volume up on a radio on his desk. Election returns
were coming in from Nebraska. Adlai III said, "How many
write-in votes have we got?"

Blair said, "Two. Cousins, I suppose."

Laughing, Adlai hurried toward the bathroom. "Hey, Dad,
how many relatives have we got in Nebraska?"

# CHAPTER II

# Background

In a cabinet in the drawing room of the Executive Mansion in Springfield, Governor Adlai Ewing Stevenson keeps a few old books, a photograph of an old family residence, and a collection of campaign buttons and ribbons from the presidential campaign of 1892, when the Democratic candidates were Grover Cleveland for President, and, for Vice-President, Adlai Ewing Stevenson, the grandfather of the present Governor and for whom he was named.

On Governor Stevenson's desk in his Statehouse office is an ornate silver inkwell presented to Vice-President Stevenson "by the Senators of Washington, D. C.," on March 4, 1897, when he was leaving office.

On the walls of Governor Stevenson's office in the Mansion hang old gilt-framed oil paintings of his Grandfather Stevenson and his father, Lewis Green Stevenson, as well as a large framed facsimile of an old document entitled, "The Autobiography of Abraham Lincoln." Governor Stevenson's great-grandfather on his mother's side, Jesse W. Fell, persuaded Lincoln to write it. The document contains a foreword by Fell, who wrote on March 20, 1872, at Normal, Illinois:

In presenting to the public a facsimile of Abraham Lincoln's Autobiography, it is due to the memory of that great man, that a

brief statement be made of the circumstances under which it was
written. In the Autumn of 1858, during the celebrated discussion
between Senator Douglas and Mr. Lincoln, I had occasion to travel
in the Middle and Eastern states, and finding there a laudable
curiosity to learn something more of the latter than was then generally known, and looking too, to the possibilities of his becoming
an available candidate for the Presidency in 1860, I applied to him
for a brief history of his early life. After repeated efforts on my part,
in December 1859, he placed in my hands a manuscript written with
that freedom and unreserve which one friend would exercise in
talking to another, and in which his peculiar conversational style
is so happily set forth. I need scarcely add that this simple unadorned
statement of his was not intended for publication, but merely to give
a few facts relating to his early history.

The "autobiography" that Lincoln wrote begins:

I was born February 12, 1809, in Hardin County, Kentucky. My
parents were both born in Virginia, of undistinguished families.
Second families, perhaps I should say. My mother, who died in my
tenth year, was of a family of the name of Hanks, some of whom
now reside in Adams, and others in Macon counties, Illinois. My
paternal grandfather, Abraham Lincoln, emigrated from Rocking-
ham County, Virginia, to Kentucky, about 1781 or 2 when, a year
or two later, he was killed by Indians, not in battle, but by stealth,
when he was laboring to open a farm in the forest. . . .

Governor Adlai Ewing Stevenson belongs to one of the minor
dynasties of American politics and public life. He is proud of
his lineage. (His wife, who divorced him a few years ago, has
been widely quoted as saying that the Stevensons worship their
ancestors like the Japanese.) On both sides of his family, his
ancestors have been traced back to pre-Revolutionary times.
They acquired money and prominence about the time of the
Civil War. They settled in central Illinois and grew up with it.
Stevenson stands in an old tradition of Midwest politics—a

tradition that embraces farming, newspaper publishing, the law, and minor wealth. But in all these fields the Stevensons have been uncommonly successful.

## ORIGINS

On his father's side of the family, the first Stevenson emigrated to America from North Ireland in 1748, settling in Pennsylvania, moving soon to a land grant in North Carolina, and serving in the American Revolution. The Stevensons were Scotch Presbyterians. One of them crossed the mountains in 1814 and settled in Christian County, Kentucky, and his son went north and arrived at Bloomington, Illinois, on July 7, 1852, taking with him his wife and children. It was one of these children, Adlai Ewing Stevenson, who subsequently became Vice-President of the United States. (He endeared himself to his fellow Democrats during Cleveland's first administration by getting rid of some forty thousand Republican postmasters, a labor for which he was nicknamed "The Headsman" and rewarded with the vice-presidential nomination. Subsequently he ran again for Vice-President, in 1900, with William Jennings Bryan. They lost.)

Vice-President Stevenson's wife, whose own ancestors had fought with George Washington and explored the Western wilderness and whose mother bore the remarkable name of Mary Peachy Fry Green, was an early and active member of the Daughters of the American Revolution, the Colonial Dames, the Women's Clubs of America, and an organizer of the forerunner of the Parent-Teachers' Association. The son born to her and the Vice-President was Lewis Green Stevenson, the father of the present Governor Stevenson.

On his mother's side, Governor Stevenson's ancestors have been traced back through eight generations of Fells to northern England. One of them emigrated to America in 1704 or 1705.

They were Quakers and settled in William Penn's colony. Jesse W. Fell went West in 1828 on foot, carrying his belongings in a knapsack. After pausing to work on an antislavery newspaper in Virginia and to study law in Ohio he reached Illinois in 1832 and became the first lawyer in Bloomington. Bloomington is a farm town 125 miles southwest of Chicago. It is the seat of McLean County which has often been said to contain the richest soil in America. It is flat land, and fat, and black.

Jesse Fell became a land speculator. He bought and sold farmlands, he founded towns all over the burgeoning central Illinois prairie, he made a fortune and lost it in the Panic of 1837 and made another. He lived in the same house as Lincoln in the old Illinois capital at Vandalia, where Lincoln was a member of the General Assembly, and he was one of the first men to conceive the idea of running Lincoln for President. The Lincoln-Douglas debates were said to have been his idea.

Jesse Fell was a Bloomington booster, helped bring the Normal College there. He founded Bloomington's first newspaper, bringing in the type and presses by flatboat and wagon. The paper failed. In 1868, with his son-in-law William O. Davis and another man, he bought the Bloomington *Pantagraph*. Davis acquired full ownership of the paper in 1871 and it soon became, as it is today, one of the most influential and valuable newspaper properties in central Illinois. Davis' daughter was the present Governor Stevenson's mother. The Governor has a twenty-three per cent interest in the *Pantagraph* and it is still the principal source of his private income.

Adlai Ewing Stevenson, the present Governor of Illinois, was born February 5, 1900, in Los Angeles, California, where his father was working as assistant general manager of a Hearst newspaper. Previously his father had acted as secretary to his own father, the Vice-President, had covered the Sino-Japanese War, and had begun his connection with William Randolph

Hearst by managing gold and copper mines in New Mexico and Arizona for Hearst's mother.

The name "Adlai" is of biblical origin. Dictionaries give its proper pronunciation as rhyming approximately with "gadfly" but most people pronounce it rhyming approximately with "gladly." The Governor pronounces it *"Ad-*lay." The name entered the Stevenson family six generations ago. Last summer when Jack Benny, the comedian, visited the Illinois State Fair, he told an audience of twelve thousand people that included the Governor, "I have just had the shock of my life. I flew across the United States bearing a lovely corsage only to discover that Adlai is not a woman's name."

Stevenson's grandfather is said to have attended a luncheon at which Mark Twain recited:

> Philologists sweat and lexicographers bray,
> But the best they can do is to call him Ad-lay.
> But at longshoremen's picnics, where accents are high,
> Fair Harvard's not present, so they call him Adlai.

## BOYHOOD IN BLOOMINGTON

In 1903, when Stevenson was three years old, his parents moved back to Bloomington. Here his father managed ten thousand acres of farmland in Indiana, Illinois and Iowa, acted as a director of a coal company, and became active in the town's public affairs. Bloomington was then as it is today a quiet county-seat town and college town, its shady streets lined with the big square frame houses that Midwest farmers like to retire to. It is a rich town. The Stevensons were a leading family. A section of town on the wrong side of the tracks is called Stevensonville, because the Stevensons once owned the land there, and busses running to that section are still marked "Stevensonville."

The Stevensons in Adlai's boyhood lived in a pleasant house in the best section of town, the east side. They moved in the best social circles.

Their orbit was by no means restricted to Bloomington. Summers they spent at Charlevoix, Michigan, a fashionable Midwest resort colony. Stevenson's grandfather had been one of the founders of the Chicago Club at Charlevoix, to which belonged many wealthy families from Chicago and its fashionable North Shore suburbs. Many of Stevenson's Chicago and North Shore connections, so important in his later life, began at Charlevoix. During his boyhood a cousin of his had a beach cottage at Charlevoix and the family stayed there or at the Belvedere Club, where his grandfather, W. O. Davis, owned a cottage. Some summers the Stevensons went to a guest ranch in Wyoming. Winters too they traveled.

Stevenson's father had attended Phillips Exeter Academy in the East and, as we have seen, had traveled widely on business; his acquaintance was a national one. Stevenson, asked recently about his family and his boyhood, said, "My father was a very delicate frail man physically, subject to migraine headaches, a family affliction which, fortunately, I have escaped. He was a very witty, amusing, and jolly man.

"My father was an early scientific farmer and farm manager. He was one of the first to take all the tenants to the University of Illinois School of Agriculture for a short course—at the expense of the landlords," he added, smiling quickly. "He was one of the first men actively interested in soybeans around here. He made planting soybeans a condition of the lease. Today soybeans is a leading crop.

"In my childhood my grandfather's health was bad, that is my Grandfather Davis, my mother's father, and in the winters we went South for his health, usually to Pass Christian or Biloxi or Florida. His family was very prominent in central Illinois.

So wherever we traveled we knew people through the two families.

"My mother was very much a mother, preoccupied with the children and their health. I recall she used to read to us in the evening from earliest childhood. Most of her reading was Greek mythology and the romantic writers like Walter Scott. There was a good deal of reading by my Grandfather Davis, when we were young, in the poets. I remember Bobby Burns was a favorite of his. I think my interest in American history came from my Grandfather Stevenson.

"Grandfather Stevenson was a very prominent and distinguished Democrat and Presbyterian. His was a very formal household. He addressed his wife as Mrs. Stevenson and she addressed him as Mr. Stevenson. He was a great raconteur, one of the great raconteurs of his day, and I think this had something to do with his political success. Well, saturated as he was with American history and a political figure, too, and my father, too, I picked up a good deal of that through the bloodstream. My father's family was Democratic and Scotch Presbyterian. My mother's family were strong Republicans and Unitarians." Stevenson has compromised: he is a Democrat and a Unitarian.

The Stevenson house in Bloomington was always full of people, many of them "distinguished Democrats," as Stevenson says. His early recollections include visits by such men as William Jennings Bryan. Other people who lived in Bloomington in those days recall receptions for celebrities and post-election soirees at the Stevenson home. Stevenson is fond of a lithograph entitled "The Lost Bet" which hangs on his office wall. Depicting a post-election scene of 1892, it shows a gentleman in top hat and frock coat paying off an election bet by pulling a wagon down a street beneath a banner lettered Grover Cleveland and Adlai E. Stevenson, their photographs flanking one of Governor John P. Altgeld of Illinois.

Stevenson's father, too, was active in politics. He traveled around Illinois to Democratic committee meetings. In 1908 he managed the unsuccessful campaign of his father, the ex-Vice-President, for Governor of Illinois. He was appointed Secretary of State of Illinois by Governor Dunne to fill a vacancy in 1914 and ran for election to the same office in 1916. "He ran way ahead of the ticket," Stevenson recalls, "but it was a year of Republican victory. I think he may have run ahead of Woodrow Wilson."

When Stevenson was twelve years old he met Wilson, who had just been elected Governor of New Jersey, during a family trip to Seabright, New Jersey. Wilson was an early idol of Stevenson's. "He was a friend of my father," Stevenson has said. "He was not only a Democrat but he was president of Princeton, where I went to school."

### AWAY TO SCHOOL

In 1912 young Stevenson made his first trip abroad. He lived in Europe a year, attending school in Switzerland. Previously he had gone to public school in Bloomington but traveling had interfered with his attendance—"I don't think I even started till I was about nine"—and his early education suffered. His parents wanted him to go East to college. He spent two years in Bloomington High School. "Then," he recalls, "I took three college entrance examinations and I don't think the aggregate scores I made were sufficient to enable me to pass any one of them. So my parents concluded that there was either something wrong with me or the schools, and shipped me off to an Eastern preparatory school." This was Choate, in Connecticut. His cousin, Davis Merwin, had gone there. "It worked very well," Stevenson recalls, "and I was able to enter Princeton two years later."

At Princeton Stevenson's main interest was the *Daily Prince-*

*tonian.* (At Choate too he had worked on the school paper and literary magazine.) He was on the editorial board of the *Daily Princetonian* for three years, managing editor in his senior year. "Made quite a bit of money for them the last year too," he said recently.

People who went to Princeton remember that he was "fairly well-known" on the campus. He was a member of the senior council and of two commencement committees. His grades were average. When the senior class voted sobriquets to its members, Stevenson showed up on four lists. In the voting for "biggest politician" he came in third, receiving 8 votes. (The winner received 124 votes and the second man 9 votes. Neither of them is prominent in politics today.) In the voting for *"thinks* he is the biggest politician" Stevenson did better: he came in second, with 28 votes to the same winner's 41. He was ranked eighteenth among those "most likely to succeed," receiving 2 votes. And he was last of 9 men (out of a class of about 325) voted "best all-around man outside athletics."

A college photograph shows Stevenson tall, slender, serious of mien, with a thin face, a high forehead, and a cleft chin, the whole effect being almost aesthetic. He traveled a good deal on vacations, spending his summers still at Charlevoix or at a Western ranch.

One man who knew him then recalls, "Steve was the one you imposed on, the one you got to do everything—he bought the theater tickets, made the travel arrangements, that sort of thing. But he never did it right. There's a story about a trip he and another fellow made to Los Angeles. Steve spent a whole day in downtown Los Angeles getting the railroad tickets. He said he had everything arranged. Turned out they had to change trains somewhere in the desert in the middle of the night and I think they ended up on different trains." Many people called him "Steve" in college, a nickname almost never heard today. His friends today call him "Adlai." A few of them call him "Ad." He was thought to be "good company on a party" but "rather conservative in his fun." Week ends he played tennis and visited the homes of college friends in the East. His closest college friends were Eastern, though he also consorted with several men from the North Shore suburbs of Chicago.

He was in the Naval Reserve. He attended the social functions that undergraduates of wealth and social position at the Ivy League colleges attend. He thought some of the affairs he was expected to attend stuffy, as, for example, Sunday evening gatherings in the homes of Bostonians who liked to play "mental games," as a friend of Stevenson's put it, after supper—"answering questions like what is the highest mountain in the world beginning with 'M'?" Stevenson graduated from Princeton in 1922. He feels a strong loyalty to Princeton. He has returned for his tenth and twenty-fifth class reunions.

Stevenson wanted to go into the newspaper business but his father wanted him to study law. He entered Harvard Law School. He left after two years. The story goes that he dropped out because of low grades. There is truth in this, but it is not the whole truth, and although correcting the story is rather painful to Stevenson for personal reasons, it ought to be done, since saying only that he flunked out of law school impugns his intelligence or diligence unfairly and calls into question his qualifications for public office, whereas the truth reflects neither credit nor discredit upon the man himself.

The truth is, as usual, complicated. In the spring of 1924 Stevenson's uncle, Hibbard O. Davis, who had for years been editing the Bloomington *Pantagraph* that his father had owned, died. Stevenson went home for the funeral. The ownership of the newspaper was in dispute between Stevenson's own family and the family of his cousins, Davis and Loring Merwin. Since the *Pantagraph* was a valuable property, this was a serious matter. The dispute arose over interpretation of the wills left by Stevenson's grandfather, William O. Davis, and uncle, Hibbard Davis. It resulted in litigation that was finally settled in the Illinois Supreme Court.

As a result of the lawsuit, Stevenson today has a twenty-three per cent stock interest in the *Pantagraph,* his sister has a twenty-three per cent interest, and the Merwin family has a majority interest. Discussing this "horrible family dispute" is painful to Stevenson. Matters have long since been mended, and during his political career Stevenson has had no stancher backer than his cousin Loring Merwin, the present editor of the *Pantagraph,* although Merwin is a Republican and his editorial policy Republican.

At the time however the families were thrown into an uproar. It was decided that Stevenson was to go into the newspaper to represent his family's interest, while Davis Merwin, his cousin, was to represent the Merwin family's interest. Stevenson went back to law school to finish out that term. Having lost a good deal of time from school he failed in two subjects.

That summer, 1924, he became an editor of the paper, together with Davis Merwin. He stayed a year and a half. He had always liked newspapering anyway, and to this day retains his affection for it. His father, however, feared that the Stevensons might lose their interest in the *Pantagraph* through the litigation then pending. If this happened, he felt, young Stevenson ought to be able to fall back on the law as a career. Furthermore, he already had invested considerable time in his law course. So Stevenson enrolled in Northwestern University Law School, commuting from Bloomington to Evanston. He received his law degree in June of 1926, passed the bar examination, and was admitted to the Illinois bar.

"Then," he says, "I thought I'd have one last fling at journalism and traveling before settling down as a lawyer," so in the summer of 1926 he went off to Europe with credentials as a foreign correspondent wangled from International News Service, the Hearst wire service. He traveled through central Europe and Scandinavia and, taking a freighter to the Black Sea, entered the Soviet Union by the back door. His purpose was to interview the then Russian Foreign Minister Georgi Vasileyvich Chicherin and, though he failed, he is rather proud of having made the trip, since the Soviet frontier was then closed and few Western Europeans or Americans were entering Russia. He remained abroad from June until midwinter, then returned to Illinois where, he says, "I concluded that all things considered I'd better forgo journalism and get to work as a lawyer."

He settled in Chicago. Chicago and its fashionable suburbs henceforward became his base.

### THE LAW AND LAKE FOREST

Many successful Americans, and especially politicians, like to claim humble origin, to pretend that they "started from scratch" and are "self-made men." They seem to feel that this will endear them to less successful men who started out with nothing and still have nothing. Adlai Stevenson is fond of recalling that he started his career as a law clerk paid $125 a month. But characteristically he does not conceal that his family and college connections helped him, both at the outset and later.

His first job was with the law firm of Cutting, Moore and Sidley. This is an old, successful, and respected law firm with offices on LaSalle Street, the heart of Chicago's financial district. It is the kind of law firm which uses a letterhead containing the names of founders and former partners long deceased.

Adlai Stevenson got a job there as a law clerk through a college connection. A classmate of his, M. Ogden West ("Og West," as Stevenson calls him), who ultimately became a partner in Cutting, Moore and Sidley, had a brother-in-law that was a partner in that firm. Since that time, 1927, Stevenson, except as we shall see for various excursions into public life, has remained at the same law firm. Its name today is Sidley, Austin, Burgess & Smith. Stevenson became a partner in the firm in 1935.

As matters have turned out Stevenson has devoted more time to public affairs than to practicing law. When he started out, however, he gave every evidence of buckling down seriously to the drudgery of the long climb upward in the law. People who knew him then remember him as a serious young man. He worked hard. He worked long hours each day. He took few vacations. He has said, "My system of working always has been to work two solid years, then talk the firm into giving me a double vacation so I could take a long trip. It is a practice I don't recommend—it means too much uninterrupted work."

He was living at 70 East Elm Street in an old brownstone mansion converted into a roominghouse, on the receding edge of the Gold Coast, Chicago's wealthiest, most exclusive residential district, on the Near North Side, a little over a mile from the Loop. He lived alone. Other young men with prospects similar to his lived in the same building and in others near by. He played squash a good deal at the old Harvard-Yale-Princeton Club and was active in the club's affairs. (It is now defunct. A former member said recently, "In its dying days it even took in people from Dartmouth.") Summers, Stevenson moved out to Lake Forest.

If there is in America an aristocracy of money and family tradition, its Midwest repository is Lake Forest. Lake Forest is the most fashionable of the string of North Shore suburbs that runs for thirty miles north of Chicago along the shore of Lake Michigan. Lake Forest is an area of mansions and large estates. The rich dwell here.

Stevenson's entree to this society was originally through his family and Charlevoix childhood connections. Later, as an undergraduate, he knew young men from Lake Forest; as a bachelor he saw them at the Harvard-Yale-Princeton Club.

Stevenson and some other young men took to renting a house in Lake Forest for the summer. They called it "The Chateau." They rented the home of the president of Lake Forest College when he moved out at the end of the school term. They stayed until school started in the fall. Most of them were young lawyers and bankers and brokers who, like Stevenson, had come to Chicago to start their business careers. Some of the men who stayed at the Chateau are dead now—Ogden West, Harry Wilmerding, and Bill Lauterbach—"They're all dead now," Stevenson says sadly, "oh, it's terrible." Others are now prominent in Chicago affairs—Walter Paepcke, chairman of Container Corporation of America; Stephen Y. Hord, partner in the banking and investment advisory firm of Brown Brothers, Harriman and Company; James F. Oates, Jr., chairman of the board and chief executive officer of the Peoples Gas Light and Coke Company.

The Chateau persisted for about fifteen years. Its membership changed continuously—somebody dropping out to get married, a new man coming along. It was a bachelor headquarters. Stevenson says, "We just rented a house and hired a cook and split expenses. Sometimes people would come out for the week end and sleep on the sofa. It was a very fluid thing. A man might stay a week or three months." A Lake Forest man said recently, "I remember dropping in there on Sunday morning and finding clothes strewn all over the place and people sleeping on the sofa. It was a shambles."

Several years they rented a different house, one called "Red Bird Cottage" on a private estate, and here they had to be more circumspect, since the daughters of the owner of the estate dropped in now and then to play cards. Evenings the young men would, as one of them, now gray, recalls, "put on our tuxedos and go calling by bicycle." They rode bicycles to catch the commuter train in the morning. Sometimes, seeing them coming a moment late, the engineer would hold the train.

The young men were all on "Miss Campbell's list." Miss Campbell was a social secretary in Chicago to whom the mothers of debutantes applied for the names of "accredited young gentlemen." "Any of us that didn't badly misbehave were on the list," one man recalls. Their social life in Lake Forest revolved around the Ontwentsia Club. Stevenson is still a member. He played a good deal of tennis and a little golf.

All this belongs to the past. Few if any young men live this way today. "Most of us at the Chateau," one of them remembers, "were either boys just starting or men a little older who had established positions in LaSalle Street that required a rather conservative social life. Most of them were operating on a careful budget. I know I was making $150 a month and I think most of the others were making about the same."

People who knew Stevenson then do not remember him as one of the gayest of his group. "I always think of Ad as a terrific worker," says one. "Of course, nearly all the young lawyers were. More so than the bankers. The lawyers were getting the seven-sixteen train in the morning and weren't coming back out till after six in the evening. No young lawyer caught the five-ten from the city. I remember a skiing week end at Charlevoix with Adlai—he worked all week end."

Stevenson's bachelor days only lasted two years. They ended December 1, 1928, when he married Ellen Borden. She was only nineteen, nine years younger than he, a dark-haired pretty girl. Borden is a prominent name in Chicago social and financial circles. The family fortune was founded on Southwest oil and Chicago taxicabs. Ellen was an outstanding debutante of the 1927-28 season, if not *the* outstanding debutante. Stevenson visited in her family's summer home on Lake Geneva in southern Wisconsin for week ends of sailing, golfing, and swimming. A friend of theirs has said, "Ellen was a brilliant wealthy prominent girl, the headliner of the debs. Adlai was a bright young lawyer from downstate, well liked by people who knew him, but not particularly well-known in Chicago. Lots of people said, 'How wonderful that he got her.' "

A man who attended Stevenson's bachelor dinner at the Harvard-Yale-Princeton Club remembers that Stevenson was the most self-possessed bridegroom-to-be that he ever had seen. Their wedding was small but "very social," held in the chapel of the Fourth Presbyterian Church on Upper Michigan Avenue. The reception was held at the bride's mother's mansion at 1020 Lake Shore Drive, across Bellevue Place from the Edith Rockefeller McCormick mansion.

The Stevensons took a six-weeks' honeymoon trip to North Africa. Returning to Chicago they took an apartment in a reconditioned brownstone on East Walton Street on the Near North Side. After a year they moved to a more imposing building at 1120 Lake Shore Drive. Their first child was born October 10, 1930, and they named him Adlai Ewing Stevenson III. They had two other sons, Borden Stevenson, born July 7, 1932, and given Mrs. Stevenson's family name, and John Fell Stevenson, born February 7, 1936, and given the name of an English ancestor of Stevenson's eight generations removed.

### MR. STEVENSON GOES TO WASHINGTON

John Gunther, the journalist, has written that Stevenson was one of "many first-class American business and professional men [who] went to Washington during the war, giving up their jobs, sacrificing their homes in some cases and their savings, to work for the United States of America and freely give every inch and ounce of themselves for victory."

Actually Stevenson's public career began eight years before Pearl Harbor, in 1933. Shortly after Franklin D. Roosevelt took office he set up the Agricultural Adjustment Administration and named as its first administrator George Peek. A young Chicagoan named Wayne Chatfield-Taylor had gone to Washington with Peek. Taylor was a friend of Stevenson's. Stevenson recalls, "Peek was looking for some young lawyers to help him out and Wayne told him about me. He said I was all hot and bothered about the plight of the farmer, I came from an old farm family at Bloomington, and Peek said, 'Hell, that's Louie Stevenson's boy—I know Louie.'" Lewis Stevenson, the present Governor's father, who had died in 1929, had worked with Peek in the 1920's when both were interested in the McNary-Haugen Bill and other farm legislation. Peek invited Stevenson to come to Washington as a member of the AAA staff and Stevenson was delighted to do so.

"Those were frenzied days in Washington," Stevenson remembers, speaking rather fondly. "I was handling special crops, writing marketing agreements, mostly for tree crops on the West Coast. The crops were ripening on the trees by the time the Act was passed. I guess I wrote more marketing agreements of that kind than anybody else. And fast, too."

He left AAA and helped organize the Federal Alcohol Control Administration. He was its assistant general counsel.

At that time the Roosevelt revolution was exploding in all directions. Washington was full of new faces. Many of them were the faces of young lawyers. This was Adlai Stevenson's baptism in public life. He was then thirty-three. And he was a Democrat.

## THE WORLD OUTSIDE

In 1935 Stevenson returned to Chicago and resumed his law practice. He bought seventy acres of land in Libertyville, a rural estate section west of Lake Forest, and built a home of advanced architecture. It was a pleasant place on the bank of the Des Plaines River, trees shading a white plank fence, grass growing lush in the meadows. Here he settled with his family, riding horseback, overseeing the farm (the actual farming was done by a hired man), handling his investments, buying and selling farmlands in Illinois, Indiana, and Iowa, and commuting to his Chicago law office. It was an extremely pleasant life, probably the happiest period in all his life. He and his wife were deeply in love. Theirs seemed an ideal existence.

He began to participate in civic affairs. His interest at first was on a social basis—men in his station of life "just do that sort of thing." An insurance executive who is today one of his two or three closest friends, Hermon Dunlap Smith, usually called "Dutch," who had known him since their boyhood summers at Charlevoix, said recently. "I remember Adlai and I went on the Home and Aid Board at the same time. They needed a few people and they asked several of us over for luncheon. Adlai and I went on the Board. I guess I was the one that got him on the Hull House Board. Those things just happen, you know." In addition to the Board of the Illinois Children's Home and Aid Society, Stevenson was on the Board of International House at the University of Chicago, served as chairman of the Civil Rights Committee of the Chicago Bar Association and as president of the Princeton Club of Chicago.

The civic activity that came to dominate all others in Stevenson's life of this period, however, and the one that may be said to have resulted, though indirectly, in his entry into politics was his membership in the Chicago Council on Foreign Relations. This was simply a group of people who enjoyed getting together to talk about a common interest, foreign affairs. Stevenson, who had traveled a good deal abroad, who had an interest in American history, who had been an admirer of the man who up till that time had probably labored more strenuously than anyone else to involve America in foreign affairs, Woodrow Wilson, was naturally drawn to such a group. Stevenson became the Council's director and president. He often delivered speeches at its meetings. And at other meetings as well. Stevenson was a graceful speaker and a skillful and entertaining toastmaster. His services were in demand. He could afford the time and money to indulge himself by giving them. In fact, there is some evidence that during the 1930's he devoted more time to speech-writing and public speaking than to his nominal profession, the law, and that during the late 1930's and the early 1940's he thought of himself primarily as a public speaker.

After Hitler invaded Poland in 1939, and the American "defense" mobilization, as it then was called, began, the questions to which nobody but the Council on Foreign Relations had previously paid much attention suddenly became matters of the utmost urgency. What had been a polite academic discussion became a rough-and-tumble brawl. That was the period of the great debate between the "isolationists" and the "interventionists."

The Midwest was then considered isolationist, both because the Chicago *Tribune* claimed to speak for the Midwest and its message was isolationism and because America First found a good deal of its support there. Stevenson was chairman of the Chicago branch of the Committee to Defend America by Aiding the Allies, a group founded by William Allen White to oppose isolationism. Stevenson organized mass meetings to persuade public opinion to the point of view of the White Committee: that aid to the Allies was not intervention but the only means possible of keeping the United States out of the war. It was in these enterprises that he became close to Colonel Frank Knox.

He had met Knox, publisher of the Chicago *Daily News,* during the 1930's. "We met in various community activities,"

Stevenson recalls. "I was a very energetic young man closely identified with him during the year immediately preceding America's entry into the war when I was active in this agitation in conflict with the America First Committee." (It is interesting to note that Stevenson describes his activities at this time as being *against* rather than *for* something.)

President Roosevelt appointed Knox, a Republican, Secretary of the Navy in 1940. Knox invited Stevenson to join his staff in Washington but then changed his mind, thinking Stevenson could be more useful in Chicago combating "isolationism." (Stevenson, characteristically, nowadays gives the story of his appointment a humorous twist. He says that after Knox had been in Washington awhile Knox telephoned him one day and said he was embarrassed to discover at every conference he attended that he was the only important personage present without his own lawyer—would Stevenson please be his lawyer?) Stevenson stayed in Chicago, representing Knox, for a year. Knox visited Chicago once a month and Stevenson would report on the then state of public opinion. "After Lend-Lease passed, he renewed his invitation to go to Washington," Stevenson remembers, "and that seemed a good place to cut off, so I went."

It was a major turning point in Stevenson's life. He gave up his law practice. He sold most of his farms because, as he said recently, "while I have nothing against absentee landlordship, I feel that the landlord should participate. I'm not trying to pass judgment on these rich men who buy farms as an inflation hedge or anything. I'm just speaking for myself. To me, it doesn't seem fair that the poor devil tenant should struggle along year after year and the landlord should not once even worry about whether he needs a new pump or new wallpaper in his house. I just felt if I couldn't be there I'd better get out altogether."

He was "special assistant" to Knox. That is, he traveled with

Knox, wrote speeches for him, occasionally delivered them, "ran errands" for him, and in general acted as his "trouble-shooter" and "handyman."

For a time the Stevensons had a house in Washington on R Street. Later in the war, when Stevenson's duties kept him away from Washington more and more, Mrs. Stevenson returned to the farm in Libertyville and Stevenson moved into an apartment in Washington.

On the week end of December 7, 1941, the Stevensons were entertaining their Lake Forest friends, Dutch Smith and his wife, in Washington. Smith recalls, "They were going to have a dinner party for us on Friday night. The whole question of war was very much in the air. Adlai was trying to settle some very difficult shipyard strike for the Navy. He and I were driving across town to a cocktail party or somewhere before dinner and he told me that a group of people in Illinois had asked him to consider running for the Senate in 1942 against Senator Brooks." Brooks was a Republican and a leading isolationist, generally considered a spokesman for the Chicago *Tribune*. "He said it was some of the old Horner group that had suggested it," that is, men close to Henry Horner, the New Deal Demo-crat-elected Governor of Illinois at the same time that Roose-velt was elected President. Smith went on, "Adlai asked me, 'Do you think it makes any sense?' I said I didn't know anything about it and besides I was a Republican. He asked me to see what I could find out about it and I said I would. It was the first time I'd ever heard Adlai express any interest in politics."

The outbreak of war that same week end ended any thoughts Stevenson had of entering politics.

Stevenson found wartime Washington enormously exciting, as did many other men who went there "to help." He saw more and more of high government officials. He met Roosevelt and traveled all over the world with Knox. He acquired experience in dealing with foreign officials that later was to prove invaluable. In 1943 he took leave from the Navy to lead the first mission dispatched to Italy by the Foreign Economic Administration after the liberation of Italy. In 1944 he went on a War Department mission to France, England, and Belgium. He was forty-four years old, urbane, educated, adroit, an excellent speaker, one of the bright youngish American advisers in the first rank below cabinet level.

In February, 1945, he was appointed special assistant to Secretary of State Edward Stettinius, Jr., and served as adviser to the United States Delegation on International Organization at the San Francisco Conference, from which came the United Nations Charter. At San Francisco Stevenson operated as liaison man between the United States Delegation and the press.

In the fall of 1945 Stevenson went to London as deputy to Stettinius, who, having resigned as Secretary of State, was United States Delegate to the Executive Committee of the United Nations Preparatory Commission. When Stettinius fell ill, Stevenson took his place, first on the Executive Committee as delegate and chairman, and then as acting delegate at the Preparatory Commission meetings which chose the United States as the permanent seat of the United Nations.

At the first meeting of the General Assembly in London in early 1946, Stevenson was senior adviser to the United States Delegation. Again in the fall of 1946, he was alternative representative to the General Assembly Delegation, dealing mainly with the committees on post-UNRRA relief and the economic reconstruction of devastated areas. And in 1947 he was alternate delegate, working this time on the Budgetary and Administrative Committee and later on the Membership Committee.

He performed all these duties with considerable distinction. His particular forte was personal negotiation. A man who observed him in London has said, "He was smooth as can be. I never saw a man handle the Russians like he did."

Senator Arthur H. Vandenberg (R., Michigan), Chairman of the Senate Committee on Foreign Relations in this period, wrote Stevenson: "I am glad you are going to the General Assembly. I want you to know—as a matter of record—that when I was asked for recommendations in connection with the United States Delegation, I put your name down as a 'must.' I wish you were devoting all of your time to our foreign affairs at a high level in the State Department."

Of Stevenson's work in London, Secretary of State James F. Byrnes wrote: "I want to thank you on behalf of the President and myself for the distinguished services you have rendered. . . . You have helped greatly to get the United Nations started as a going concern."

# CHAPTER III

# The 1948 Campaign

SEVERAL people who took part in Adlai Stevenson's 1948 campaign for Governor of Illinois have said, looking back on it, "It was an absolutely incredible campaign." It sure was. Probably the most incredible thing about it was that Stevenson was in it.

In Washington and New York he had acquired a modest reputation during the war but not among politicians.

In Illinois, he was virtually unknown.

Illinois politicians dwell in a dark jungle he never had approached.

His own roots were in Lake Forest and Bloomington. Lake Forest contains 7,819 people, Bloomington 34,163, and nearly all of them are Republicans. Stevenson was a Democrat.

Here matters stood at the beginning of 1947. A year later Stevenson was the Democratic Party's nominee for Governor. And a year after that he was inaugurated at Springfield.

Let us inquire briefly into how this came about.

It started as uplift. Louis A. Kohn, a bouncy stocky well-to-do Chicago lawyer, then thirty-nine and a partner in Mayer, Meyer, Austrian & Platt, one of Chicago's leading law firms, got out of the Army in 1946 with the rather vague idea that he wished there were some way to get Adlai Stevenson elected

Senator from Illinois. Kohn had met Stevenson during the 1930's, first when both men, as lawyers, were representing clients with common interests and later when both were attending meetings of the Chicago Council on Foreign Relations. During his three war years in the Pacific, Kohn read newspaper accounts of Stevenson's work for Secretary Knox. Kohn recalls, "While I was overseas in some god-forsaken spot I got to wondering why I was here. And I made up my mind if I ever got back home I'd try to do something about it. I began wondering, 'Who in Illinois would be the kind of a man to go to the Senate that would supply the world leadership we're going to need?' "

Back home in 1946 Kohn renewed his acquaintance with Stevenson and heard him make speeches at the Chicago Bar Association and the Council on Foreign Relations, speeches based on Stevenson's experiences in World War II. Kohn was greatly impressed. One day he cornered Stevenson at the Bar Association and said, "I'd like to talk to you about something. This may sound silly to you. But it seems to me you're the type of man that ought to run for high office." Stevenson was interested and suggested they have lunch. But Lou Kohn was no politician. As Kohn has said, "I'd been interested in politics like any other citizen but I didn't have time."

Now Kohn was not the first to get the idea that Stevenson would make a good senator. As we have seen, others had suggested it as early as 1941. But Kohn was by all odds the most persistent. "Kohn is a bulldog," one of his associates has said. "Once he gets hold of an idea he never lets go. And he always looks like he's trying to do sixteen things at one time so you feel sorry for him and offer to help. That's the way he gets people to do things for him."

Kohn saw Stevenson from time to time. He kept badgering Stevenson with letters and phone calls until Stevenson finally told his old friend Dutch Smith, "Lou Kohn is driving me crazy. He's determined that I run for the Senate. He calls me on the telephone. I don't know what to say to him. You talk to him." Smith had lunch with Kohn.

Now Smith is a Republican. He lives in a lake-front mansion in Lake Forest. He is a director and executive vice-president of Marsh and McLennan, one of the biggest if not the biggest insurance brokerage firms in America. He is wealthy. He and his wife are active in civic and charitable affairs. He is an intelligent man of wide-ranging interests, a student of Midwest history, a collector of Americana. He is one of Stevenson's closest friends. They met when they were boys at Charlevoix. They maintained their friendship at college, while beginning their business careers, and later in philanthropic activities.

Smith has said, "Most of Adlai's friends had always assumed he'd go into politics sooner or later. Mostly because of his family background, I guess. He has a very strong family feeling and I think he always had vague feelings about carrying on his family's political tradition."

At this time Stevenson was undecided about his future: whether to accept an appointive post in the State Department, to seek elective office, or to return to the Sidley law firm.

At their first lunch together, Kohn and Smith found that they agreed on foreign policy and on Stevenson's fitness for the Senate but there seemed little prospect that they could do anything about it; Smith had important connections in the financial district and Kohn in the law, but neither had more than a nodding acquaintance with any politician of importance. They met again, this time with Steve Mitchell, another lawyer. Mitchell had served in the State Department during the war and was a friend of Stevenson's and of Kohn's. These were the three men who got the original Stevenson boom started that spring of 1947—Kohn, Smith, and Mitchell.

Kohn began writing letters. He wrote to almost everybody he

knew. He procured from Stevenson a list of Stevenson's friends and he wrote to them. He wrote mostly to newspaper editors and lawyers in downstate Illinois as well as in Chicago. To all he said the same thing—that he and a group of Stevenson's friends had embarked on a campaign to get the senatorial nomination for Stevenson, that they had "sounded out a large number of people and the response is universally favorable," that they would appreciate help in investigating "the sentiment of influential Democrats in your area" and obtaining the names of other people to contact. All these letters sounded a good deal more confident than Kohn, Smith, or Mitchell felt.

Loring Merwin, Stevenson's cousin and editor of the *Pantagraph*, undertook to explore the sentiment of downstate newspaper editors.

The response to all this was mixed and sometimes peculiar. One man wrote from downstate:

Of course I feel that all good Democrats and good citizens should rally to the support of Mr. Stevenson for any important office he may seek, and I will be glad to do anything I can to promote his interests. I find it difficult, however, to give you the names of Democrats whom you should contact in this part of the state. There are a lot of Democrats down here and I can't very well select a dozen or 15 as being more prominent or active than others. If you will let me know the types of Democrats whom you wish to contact and advise me how you expect to reach them and about how many names you wish, I shall be glad to try to help you.

A Springfield editor, V. Y. Dallman, wrote:

I am eager to co-operate. . . . Certainly the sentiment is quite favorable in this area where the name Stevenson is the symbol of genuine Democracy, fine Americanism and victory.

An embittered downstate man wrote:

The first time I am in Chicago I will be glad to visit with you and your associate. You understand, however, that I am out of politics and that means OUT.

A less bitter but equally discouraged man wrote:

As to the Stevenson candidacy, I do not believe he is very well known in this area. . . . The political situation in this county, as regards the Democrats, is one of lethargy. This area was spoiled during the lush years of power. . . .

Kohn and Smith were obliged to report to Stevenson that he was virtually unknown downstate. Stevenson was not surprised. During much of this time Stevenson was in New York attending the meeting of the UN General Assembly. He left Kohn, Smith, and Mitchell pretty much to themselves.

Kohn kept on writing to people and talking to everybody that would listen. Smith applied to Milburn P. Akers, political editor of the Chicago *Sun-Times,* the newspaper opposed to the *Tribune* and owned by Marshall Field, who is a friend of Stevenson's, for his opinion of Stevenson's senatorial candidacy. (He misspelled Akers' name.) Akers responded favorably.

Greatly encouraged, Kohn, Smith and Mitchell formed a Stevenson-for-Senator Committee. One of its most active members was Mrs. Edison Dick, prominent Lake Forest clubwoman and wife of Edison Dick, a Republican, an officer and member of the board of directors of A. B. Dick & Company. Mrs. Dick and her husband are still among Stevenson's closest friends. He often visits them in Lake Forest.

Other members of the committee were prominent Chicago lawyers, businessmen, financiers, and socialites, plus a few intellectuals. Many were Republicans, such as William McCormick Blair, Jr., a wealthy young lawyer. Blair helped organize a Republicans-for-Stevenson Committee. (Blair and two other of those early backers have since joined the Stevenson administration—Blair is one of Stevenson's administrative assistants; Walter T. Fisher, a Winnetka lawyer, is head of the Illinois Commerce Commission; and Walter V. Schaefer, a Northwestern University law professor, became Stevenson's administrative assistant and later was elected to the Illinois Supreme Court.)

Kohn began contacting various newspaper and magazine writers, usually so awkwardly and with such obvious sincerity of purpose that they felt sorry for him. Small articles about Stevenson began to appear. Kohn kept wiring and writing frantically to Stevenson in New York, urging him to contact this magazine or that press agent. Stevenson's responses lacked the frantic drive of Kohn's, seemed graceful and aloof.

Stevenson declined a job in the State Department offered him by Secretary Marshall. ("As you know, this is the second time and the second Secretary that has tried to seduce me with this job and I am now engaged in trying to help them find a suitable person.")

Stevenson announced that he would accept the nomination for the Senate. Presently he wrote Kohn: "Many thanks for all the clippings. I get the faint impression that all of Illinois are not rising for 'Stevenson,' which, however, is about what I expected."

Kohn kept clipping newspapers until they overflowed his office. His habit of accumulating clippings and thrusting them onto people has become a legend among the men around Stevenson.

Once when Smith returned from a business trip to California on a train that was two hours late, he found Kohn awaiting him. Smith, late for an appointment, tried to hurry on, but Kohn undismayed trotted at his side, saying insistently, "Dutch, I just want to mention three things."

Smith hastened on through the Northwestern Railroad station.

"One, here's a draft of a letter we're going to send out." (The letter said that Illinois needed Stevenson in the Senate and that interested persons should urge his nomination upon Democratic Party leaders.) "Now," Kohn continued, "that's settled. Second, will you talk to Marshall Field about getting up some enthusiasm?"

Smith nodded. He was almost to the station exit.

"And will you raise three thousand dollars?"

Smith stopped and stared at him.

Kohn said, "Here are three names. You can get one thousand dollars from each. Adlai gave them to me."

"Oh," Smith said, rather dubiously. He knew the people. He promised to talk to them. Recently Smith recalled, "Those three people were all old friends of Adlai's. They didn't give a penny. For years they had been telling him that if he'd get into politics they'd support him financially. It was all cocktail party talk. In fact, just the other day we were talking about raising campaign funds for this year, 1952, and he suggested those same three names. I've gotten so I'm embarrassed to tell him. I just nod and forget it. Adlai's so sort of trusting."

Possibly because he was incensed at those people's refusal, Smith began to contact friends of his own, soliciting pledges of financial support if Stevenson were nominated. He had some success. Stevenson wrote to Kohn in November:

Thanks for your letter and the enclosures. While in the office on Wednesday, I noted a large stack of 100 or more of these reprints which had evidently been sent me in August and which I had overlooked. . . .

Yesterday [a Chicago politician] telephoned me . . . and seemed surprisingly optimistic with respect to myself. I hardly know why unless it has to do with larger campaign contributions. The latter is not a wholly reassuring basis for selection.

I will write to my friend in Bloomington about speaking there although the prospect of another speech is a little more than I can face at the moment!

> Sincerely,
> ADLAI

P.S. Please note the enclosed telegram. I don't know Mr. _____ or what it is all about nor am I anxious to spend my first Saturday at home with a stock show. If you know the man or anything about it, you might let me have your advice. I expect to be home Wednesday or Thursday at the latest.

P.P.S. I wish I wasn't getting so cold on this whole political business.

It was no wonder that Stevenson felt uncertain. Throughout this whole campaign, which had gone on now for almost a year, one element had been missing: a politician. They had of course contacted a number of politicians, including the then Democratic State Chairman, George Kells, and had received some encouragement from Kells and others. But they had not succeeded in getting the avowed support of any politician of the first rank.

The politicians were uncommitted to any candidate. They were, as they say, "waiting to see how things develop."

In Cook County, the man who makes things "develop" is Colonel Jacob M. Arvey. Arvey was and is the boss of the old Kelly-Nash machine in Cook County. This machine has for years been considered widely and rightly to be one of the most powerful, corrupt, and successful political machines in America. It is one of the few Democratic big-city machines that has survived the national political upheavals of recent years that have wrecked other similar machines, such as those run by Hague in New Jersey, Pendergast in Kansas City, and Crump in Memphis.

One of the principal reasons for its survival is Colonel Arvey's great skill and his acute insight into the public temper. The year of the Stevenson boom, 1947, Arvey had prevailed upon Ed Kelly to relinquish the mayoralty of Chicago and had selected Martin Kennelly, an honest businessman, to replace him. (Kennelly was elected. Nobody has yet impugned Kennelly's honesty. But he is no longer considered a reformer.) Arvey's critics say that Arvey accepted Kennelly, Stevenson, and Senator Paul Douglas as his candidates in 1947 only because he had to do so to save his machine from defeat. Arvey's friends say he did so because he was another man who returned chastened and uplifted from the war, determined to give Chicago and Illinois good government.

It was one of the ironies of politics that the mayoralty campaign of early 1947, when Arvey was supporting honest Martin Kennelly, was the campaign in which the Chicago *Tribune* lambasted Arvey more cruelly than ever before. To people who believed the *Tribune,* Arvey had horns. By and large, people who live in Lake Forest and other North Shore suburbs do believe the *Tribune.*

We are therefore about to witness a pretty tableau, for now in November of 1947 a delegation of Lake Forest and North Shore citizens waited upon Colonel Arvey to urge upon him the desirability of Adlai Stevenson as the Democratic nominee for Senator. Dutch Smith recalls, "We had an appointment at Colonel Arvey's office. We told him why we thought Adlai would make a good senator. He listened to us very courteously and then said, 'I would agree that Stevenson would make a very good senator'—of course he knew him hardly at all—'but you've got to get elected. Douglas is much better known.' " Paul Douglas, a former University of Chicago professor who had served in the Chicago City Council before being wounded in the war, had been campaigning strenuously for the senatorial nomination for months. "Colonel Arvey said, 'Douglas has been working all summer downstate. He is much better known than Stevenson and I feel he would make a better candidate.'"

At that time the common talk was that Douglas wanted to be Governor of Illinois but that the machine Democrats were afraid he'd spoil things for them at Springfield. They wanted him on their ticket for his prestige but they wanted him in the Senate, where he could wrestle with national and foreign affairs, leaving to them local and state matters, including, presumably, patronage and boodle.

Smith and his friends felt keenly the weakness of their own position: that they were amateurs, not insiders, and that this was an insiders' show.

At this juncture Smith happened to make a business trip to New York and whom should he see in the club car of the Twentieth Century Limited but Arvey, sitting alone. Smith recalls, "I'd only seen him that one time. But I went over and sat down beside him and recalled myself to him, told him I'd been in to see him a little while ago about Adlai Stevenson. I said, 'I'd like to talk to you a little more about him.' I made it sound casual. We'd been breaking our necks trying to get five minutes alone with Arvey. He invited me to go ahead and I did.

"Colonel Arvey said, 'Well, I don't know—a fellow was telling me the other day I'd better lay off Stevenson, that he went to Oxford.'" (Anglophobia is a *Tribune* trait that Arvey, as a politician, had to consider.) "I told him I knew Adlai pretty well and I was pretty sure he hadn't gone to Oxford but I suggested the best thing to do would be to ask Adlai. Colonel Arvey said that'd be fine. We talked awhile and he asked when I was going back to Chicago. I told him Thursday. He said he would be on the same train and invited me to have dinner with him."

As soon as Smith got to New York he wired Stevenson, asking

for a telegram denying that he had gone to Oxford. Stevenson replied by wire: "NEVER WENT TO OXFORD NOT EVEN TO ETON."

Smith boarded the Century for the return trip in high spirits. He met Arvey in the club car and they had a drink. Smith remembers, "The gist of our conversation was, Arvey was saying the Democrats were having a terrible time finding a candidate for Governor. They had two good candidates for Senator—Douglas and Stevenson—but they only needed one. He wanted a businessman for Governor, 'somebody of the Kennelly type,' Arvey said. He said the man couldn't be a Republican but he didn't have to be a professional Democrat. I told him, 'There's a guy right here on this train that would be a good one. Jim Knowlson. President of Stewart Warner. Do you want to ask him?' Arvey said, 'Sure.' Knowlson was sitting in the club car too so I went over and asked him, 'Do you want to be Governor of Illinois? Arvey's looking for a candidate.' Jim said, 'I'm not going to be a Democrat this year—we need a change.' He was sitting with another fellow I knew so I asked him too but he said he was a Republican. I went back to Arvey and told him that the one who was a Democrat wasn't interested and the one who was interested wasn't a Democrat. He said, 'That's the trouble.' Then we went in to dinner. Had breakfast together too. And I kept talking about Adlai."

Arvey asked, "Is there a Mrs. Stevenson?"

"Yes," Smith said.

"Do you know her?"

"Sure. She's a very charming attractive person."

"Do you think she'd be an asset to his campaign?"

"Very definitely. She's friendly, entertaining, a charming hostess. She'd do a good job. Do you want to meet her?"

"Yes."

"Why don't you come out to the house Sunday? I'll have them both there."

Arvey said he had an appointment with Mayor Kennelly to go over the city budget but would try to rearrange his schedule.

Back in Chicago Smith told Mr. and Mrs. Stevenson of the plan, then wrote a letter to Arvey, formalizing the invitation, giving detailed instructions on how to reach the Smith house, which is situated in Lake Forest on the lake at the end of a private road—"In case you should get lost for any reason, the best plan would be to go to the Walgreen Drugstore in the center of Lake Forest and telephone us"—and again urging upon Arvey several businessmen as gubernatorial material.

The Sunday lunch at Smiths was a success. "We had a very nice time," Smith recalls. "Adlai had spoken at Champaign and barely got there. Ellen—" Mrs. Stevenson "—made several observations about Douglas and the issues, she's a smart gal, quite knowing. Of course, at that time we all thought Arvey really wanted to meet her. I know now that what he actually wanted to do was look over Adlai.

"Well, in a few days Arvey called me and told me he was with Senator Lucas," then Senator from Illinois, majority leader in the Senate, and since defeated for re-election, "and asked me if I could bring Adlai over. He didn't mention his name over the phone—those politicians are always so mysterious —he just said, 'Can you get your friend and come over here?' I told him sure. I called Adlai. Adlai said he was on his way to lunch. I told him he had to do this. He said he had an engagement for lunch. I told him if he wanted to run for the Senate he'd better change his luncheon plans." Stevenson did and impressed both Arvey and Lucas favorably.

During the next few days—it was the Christmas season in 1947—Arvey talked to Smith several times. Finally he told him flatly that Douglas was going to run for the Senate and that Stevenson could have the nomination for Governor. Smith was sure Stevenson would not want to run for Governor, since all his background and interests bore much more directly on foreign affairs than on Illinois affairs, but he suggested that Arvey make the offer direct to Stevenson. Arvey agreed to do so on a Saturday morning.

The three of them met in Smith's office. Stevenson told Arvey he was interested only in the Senate. Arvey was equally frank: Douglas was their man for the Senate. Would Stevenson be their man for Governor?

Stevenson played for time. He said he'd never thought of himself as Governor, didn't know what to say. He asked, "If I should do this and be elected, would I be entirely free on my appointments?"

Arvey replied, "As far as your major appointments go, I wouldn't even make a suggestion if you asked me to. As to the rank and file, you'll have to get help somewhere—you won't know enough people to fill all the jobs—and if you need help I'll give it to you."

(Smith now says, "And Arvey has never broken his word on that.")

Stevenson asked for a few days to think it over. Arvey agreed.

A thirty-man Democratic slate-making committee was to meet in a few days. In the interval Arvey called Smith and said, "I can't understand it. Do you think Mrs. Stevenson is persuading him not to take it?"

"No," Smith said. "She told me she wanted him to. But I'll ask him."

"Well," Smith recalls, "I telephoned Adlai but he was attending a performance of the Princeton Triangle Club. I asked his wife how she felt and she said she'd prefer Springfield to Washington. So I called Arvey back and reported this. I thought I'd better not tell the Democratic politicians that Adlai was at the Triangle Club or they'd think he was a cream puff for sure so

I just told Arvey he was at the theater and they couldn't reach him."

Arvey was becoming impatient. Stevenson was reluctant. He advanced one objection after another. One was that he wanted the support of Mayor Kennelly. But Kennelly was supporting another man. Smith and Mitchell called on Kennelly. "Kennelly was adamant," Smith recalls. Finally Arvey told Smith he would await Stevenson's decision until noon the next day but no longer—the slate had to be made up.

Smith went to Stevenson's office at 9:00 A.M. Smith recalls, "The poor guy was in terrible shape. He only had till noon to make up his mind. He didn't know what to do. I told him, 'Adlai, I think you've got to look at it this way. This is a bad year for the Democrats. Everybody figures it's a terrible year. You can't get exactly what you want. But you've all your life had your interest in a political career. You've got to take it now or not at all. If you say no when they need you, they won't take you when they don't need you. This is not a decision on whether to run for Governor or not. It's a decision to have a political career or go back to the law.' "

Stevenson can be stubborn. He said, "Well, I won't do it if I can't count on Kennelly's support."

Smith said, "What choice has he? Where else can he go? It'll be either you or Green." (Dwight Green was the Republican Governor running for re-election.)

Stevenson said, "I'm bothered." And paced the office. Smith recalls, "He kept saying that over and over, 'I'm bothered.' I finally told him I'd try to find out what Kennelly would do. I hotfooted it over to see a friend of mine, Ned Brown, at the First National Bank who's a friend of Kennelly's. The clock was ticking away. Ned said the fellow closest to Kennelly is Jim Forgan. He called in Forgan. I told him the situation. He

picked up the phone and called Kennelly. Kennelly was in a
Council meeting and couldn't get out till one o'clock. I told him
to leave word for him to call, then I went back to Adlai. I told
him, 'I can't get a definite answer but at least we've accomplished this much—Kennelly knows you're interested, you've
shown your respect for his opinion. And he hasn't any other
place to go—he'll have to support you.' Of course," Smith adds,
"Adlai was wiser than I. To me it was unthinkable that Kennelly
would sulk in his tent through the whole campaign. But that
was exactly what he did do." It is hard to remember today, when
Kennelly has slipped so badly in public esteem, how eminent
was his position during that first year of his in office.

Stevenson kept hesitating. Finally he said, "Well, I guess if
I'm going to do it I have to do it. But I sure hate to."

"And so," says Smith, "I went back to my office and he telephoned Arvey and said he'd do it. And then we tried to get
going on the campaign."

### THE CAMPAIGN

Stevenson's campaign looked like something run by the Rover
Boys. Headquarters was a barren office in a downtown office
building next door to that housing the Chicago *Tribune's* Loop
office. Two girls, Pat Dowling and Carol Evans, answered the
phone, wrote letters, and ran the mimeograph. (Miss Evans is
still Stevenson's private secretary.) Kohn kept telephoning
people and arranging things. Well-meaning Lake Forest socialites came down to headquarters to try to help but accomplished
little.

The campaign manager was Jim Mulroy, a beefy old-time
Chicago newspaperman left over from the merger of the
Chicago *Sun* and *Times*. He persuaded Bill Flanagan, a young
newspaperman turned press agent, to help out. Flanagan, today
Stevenson's press secretary, recalls, "My God, they didn't have

any organization. They didn't have anybody doing their writing. I'd go over every night and Saturdays and Sundays to do it. It was the most disorganized effort I ever saw."

The campaign proceeded in an atmosphere of frantic confusion. The Rover Boys would gather to worry. Many men who pretended to inside political knowledge were derisive. Stevenson, they said, was a sacrificial lamb. After all, it was Dewey's year, wasn't it? The Cook County Democrats had simply set up Stevenson for the slaughter. Why else would they take a man like Stevenson? Sometimes the Rover Boys half-believed it. Always there were dark rumors afoot that "the organization" was dragging its feet, selling them out. "We didn't know," Kohn recalls, "that they *never* get going till October."

The campaign was run on a shoestring. Kohn had enthusiastically estimated they would have no difficulty raising $250,000. They didn't raise $100,000. (Probably five times that much—a half-million dollars—was spent in behalf of Green.) Smith recalls, "Once Stevenson called me and said unless we could raise some more funds we'd have to close the office, we couldn't pay the rent. He put in a good deal of his own money. His sister probably put in a couple of thousand. We felt it was a perfectly hopeless thing. I'd see somebody at the club, maybe my friend or his friends, and say, 'Here's a nice decent guy—you've got to give a fellow like that some support. We all keep talking about getting good men in government. Well, here's a fellow willing to make the sacrifices.' But many of Stevenson's Republican friends wouldn't contribute—they were sure of a Dewey landslide."

One rich man sent Smith a check with a note saying,

I guess Adlai Stevenson knows that I am not a New Dealer and not a Democrat, but on account of friendship for you and for him, I enclose a check for $100 to your order as treasurer of Adlai's campaign. If Adlai were running for Senator on the Republican ticket it would please me tremendously. . . . On account of domestic problems I am terribly worried about having any more Democrats in the House or Senate than we have to have, and I guess you feel that same way.

However, there are a great many advantages in having an honest man like Adlai in public office, regardless of party. . . .

Also I kid you a good deal about being a "king maker," but I appreciate the fact that you are doing an unselfish thing when you put your time in on such a venture.

The enclosed check is to be credited anonymously.

Stevenson worried a great deal about the campaign's finances. (He always worries a great deal about money—his own, the State's, anybody's.) He kept sending notes to Smith, suggesting potential sources of contributions. Once he suggested a devious method of approaching a rich man through his wife.

Behind all this financial confusion and stringency of course was a bedrock fact: Stevenson didn't want any dirty money. Political campaigns in Illinois are very often financed by gangsters, contractors, or others who hope to profit by the election results. Stevenson was determined to avoid any such alliances, and his determination was expressed not only where it might be expected in his public speeches but also in private notes to Smith as when, in a long worried letter about the lack of campaign funds, he said offhandedly, "I am, of course, trying to avoid taking any money which would leave me with any possible embarrassing commitments." Once he sent Smith a bill with a note attached: "Dutch—Another bill against our feeble treasury! AES."

The press agent was obliged to quit because there were no funds to pay him. Creditors pressed the Rover Boys. Mulroy wrote Smith,

Will you be good enough to sign the attached check which I can rush over to the radio agency? ———— and ———— are insistent upon having an additional thousand by noon tomorrow. Frankly, this is very irritating and embarrassing to me and if I do not have the additional thousand by noon I will probably have to call upon you for help. Meantime, here's hoping that the morning's mail will bring us good luck.

Once Smith sent Stevenson a check and received this note:

DEAR DUTCH:

I have opened the envelope—staggered—fainted—recovered! God bless you!

Yours,
ADLAI

So confused was the campaign that the audit of the funds was not completed until May 26, 1949, when Stevenson had been in office five months.

The campaign was a very long one. Although as we have seen Stevenson had been reluctant to undertake it, once he did undertake it he worked at it day and night for ten months. He opened his campaign with a Jackson Day speech to the party faithful at Springfield on February 21, 1948. And he never stopped running until election day.

The *Tribune* cartooned him as an amusing little boy and a "striped-pants diplomat." The little boy label got nowhere but some of the striped-pants diplomat smear stuck; indeed, it may be in part at least responsible for a false impression of Stevenson that long persisted, that he is aloof and cold.

This caricature may have stung him. Early in the campaign he lowered the intellectual caliber of his speeches to an almost ostentatiously low level, as when, to a gathering of Chicago machine men, he said of Governor Green: "Since then the august Governor has been racing up the turnpike with his shirttail on fire."

Campaigning was hard work for Adlai Stevenson. He found it

far different from delivering lofty addresses before polite, intelligent, sympathetic audiences. He worked hard at his speeches. He traveled all over the State, moving ceaselessly, often delivering several speeches a day. Politicians were a little surprised to find that people seemed to like him. The diplomat taint did less harm than they had feared, even in the River Wards of Chicago. Stevenson is a remarkably adaptable man. His campaign speeches show a wide range of quality—windy, low-level campaign oratory to the precinct captains, tightly reasoned attacks on the Green administrations' sins to downstate public audiences, large folksy talks to farmers, speeches charged with genuine emotion to minority groups, cold technical talks on taxes to taxpayers' associations. (One talk on taxes at Oak Park, a suburb of Chicago, could serve as a model of its kind.)

He promised:

—to stop corruption in state purchasing.

—to take the State Police out of politics.

—to take mine inspection out of politics and tighten up the mining laws.

—to work for a constitutional convention.

—to work for FEPC.

—to increase state financial aid to the common schools.

—to work for increased state aid to cities.

—to increase efficiency and work for economy.

—to eliminate payroll parasites.

—to prevent tax increase.

—to take road-building out of politics, and institute a rebuilding program.

—to improve the care of patients in state hospitals.

But in the main he did not campaign for a positive program—he campaigned *against* Green. Governor Green, who was seeking a third term, had himself come into office as a reformer, one of the prosecutors of Al Capone, the vigorous young vote-getter who once had almost beaten Ed Kelly for Mayor of Chicago, the apostle of righteousness bent on throwing out the Democrats who, in Governor Horner's second term, had become fat and lazy and crooked. Many people who opposed Green publicly admit privately that his intentions were good and that he accomplished a number of good things. He aspired to the presidency, however, an ambition that the *Tribune* supported so zealously that Green became known as the *Tribune's* errand boy. Distracted by visions of the White House and anxious to maintain political tranquility, Green allowed his own machine to run away with him. By the 1948 campaign his administration had become one of the most corrupt, inefficient, and ineffectual in recent Illinois history.

The Centralia coal mine had blown up, killing 111 miners, and during the ensuing investigations it had transpired that Green's coal mine inspectors had been soliciting campaign contributions from the coal mine operators. The state payroll had ballooned. On it were many men who did nothing but draw their pay. There had been scandals in state purchasing of supplies and land. The roads were in terrible shape. Taxes were up, services down. Grafters and chiselers were everywhere.

And in mid-campaign, during a complicated investigation of the murder of one of the Shelton gang at Peoria, politicians belonging to Green's machine procured the criminal indictment (dismissed after the election) of a reporter for the St. Louis *Post-Dispatch*, Green's opponent. This raised the issue of freedom of the press. Several Republican newspapers already had deserted Green but now they attacked as well as deserted him. Lou Kohn has estimated that the Shelton scandal was worth

200,000 votes, and though this is probably an exaggeration, the scandal surely had a great effect.

Stevenson capitalized on all this. He has an unerring eye for chinks in an opponent's armor. He took careful aim and struck hard. When he spoke in Bloomington he was folksy but he attacked Green forthrightly, and people rose and applauded. A reporter wrote, "A new political star has been born." As the campaign went on, he got better. The cartoon caricatures no longer bothered him. He kept his eye on Illinois, refusing to be distracted by the "internationalist" attack of his opponent. He crisscrossed the State many times. His stock in trade was, "I am not a politician, I am a citizen." People liked it.

Coal miners supported him because of Centralia. Farmers liked him because of his work with AAA and his family background in farming. He had the big-city machines. He had the support of national figures like Mrs. Eleanor Roosevelt. In Chicago he had the support of university people and members of the Independent Voters of Illinois, a group affiliated with the Americans for Democratic Action. He had the support of North Shore Republicans, some of whom thought it would be nice to have one of their own kind in Springfield but others simply people fed up with the Green machine. He had labor support, for labor had agreed with him on foreign policy before Pearl Harbor, and he promised state government reform.

Above all he had probity. He was righteous, he was correct, he was rich, he knew little of politics but much of common honesty. He had come to straighten out the mess. In the coal towns, in the farm towns, he talked to the people quietly, persuasively, offering his talents. They paid heed. He didn't dress as they did, he spoke with an "Eastern" accent. But he was upright. He seemed a reasonable man. They would vote for him.

Dutch Smith remembers election night: "Adlai voted in Libertyville, then came over here to the house and we motored into town to his mother-in-law's for dinner. It was an awful time. I didn't think he had a chance. We tried to make small talk but it was impossible. We called up some precincts and newspapers. The first returns looked pretty good but they were from Chicago—we expected to do pretty well in Chicago. Around eight or eight-thirty we went down to his headquarters.

"Out in front on the sidewalk there was a boy selling the *Tribune*. The headline said Dewey had beaten Truman by a landslide. Adlai didn't say anything. He didn't look disturbed. I began to realize that this guy had thought all along he was going to win. The headquarters was crowded but quiet. Several people said it looked like we'd lost. Adlai bet one thousand dollars at four to one that he'd won. He's not a betting man, either. We went into his office.

"And I never realized till right then that he had thought all along he'd get elected and he still thought so. Well, the returns started coming in. Good returns. He kept saying, 'Tell them to stay at the polls.'" In previous elections ballots had been stolen and elections lost. "But they were all Chicago. And then the downstate returns began coming. Counties that hadn't gone Democratic for years had gone for Adlai. We sat there absolutely dumbfounded. And Adlai was the only one not surprised. He was sitting in his little corner office. You know what he was doing? Rewriting his acceptance speech. His *acceptance* speech!"

Stevenson was elected Governor of Illinois by the largest plurality in Illinois history. He led his ticket. He carried Illinois by 572,067 votes. Truman carried it by only 33,612. Truman might have lost Illinois, a pivotal state, had it not been for Stevenson.

Of Stevenson's plurality of 572,067, 546,424 came from Cook County. To pile up the remaining 25,643 downstate, where a

Democratic candidate seldom wins at all, he carried 48 out of 101 counties.

The crowd at the inaugural ball on January 10, 1949, was the gayest in years. It was composed of ward leaders from the Chicago River Wards, downstate townsfolk, and Lake Forest socialites.

# CHAPTER IV

# Governor of Illinois

WHEN Adlai Stevenson was elected Governor of Illinois in 1948, "good-government people" who had voted for him congratulated themselves and newspapers proclaimed "a new era." Newspapers have a way of proclaiming a new era every time they win an election. But Stevenson's accession did seem to hold great promise.

It would be surprising if an administration begun in such high hopes did not disappoint.

State government has become huge and complicated. A complete review of the Stevenson administration is beyond the scope of this book. Let us, however, observe how his mind and methods operate on some of Illinois' problems.

A governor is really three people. He is the chief executive officer of the state, and as such he must run the executive departments and propose (and sometimes veto) legislation. Those are constitutional duties. But the governor is also the titular head of the government and so he must welcome visiting dignitaries to the state, must pitch the first baseball of the spring, and most importantly must make numerous speeches to the people, explaining what, as chief executive officer, he is up to. And finally the governor is the titular head of his own political party.

First, let us see how Stevenson organized his administration.

Carl McGowan, a young lawyer who today is probably Stevenson's closest adviser, said recently, "Stevenson didn't take over a going concern. He took over an operation that—well, I suppose government had come as close to a full stop in Illinois as we've ever seen. Just compare taking over New York after it had been run by Lehman and Roosevelt and Smith and taking over Illinois after eight years of Green. We've had a hell of a low tradition of government here in Illinois."

Between his election and his inauguration Stevenson worked on his legislative program and his appointments. Sometimes he hid out in a Loop hotel, sometimes in the homes of friends.

Dutch Smith recalls, "He had to start from scratch. I remember one evening right after the election he and Wally Schaefer came here to the house to get started." Walter V. Schaefer was a professor of law at Northwestern University, one of the "college crowd" that had worked for Stevenson's election. "Walter brought along a copy of the law. We didn't even know what jobs there were to be filled. We sat down with the law and made a list of departments that people had to be appointed to head. Applications for jobs started coming in and we started building files on them."

Smith laughed. "I remember the day after the election Adlai got about 250 telegrams urging him to appoint a man named Schwartz to head the Conservation Department. We were very suspicious. It sounded like some political deal. But when we investigated we found that the telegrams were from sportsmen's clubs and this guy Schwartz was all right. Adlai appointed him and he's done a fine job."

The heads of Illinois' thirteen departments constitute a governor's cabinet.

Characteristically, Stevenson chose them slowly. He took office with less than half a cabinet of his own choosing—the rest were holdovers from the Green administration, to be replaced gradually. The hostile *Tribune* thought this commendable.

By and large Stevenson has tried to appoint to his cabinet not political hacks but men who know something about the departments they run. Many of his cabinet members are successful businessmen. They include Republicans. Some are rich men who don't need to make money at state expense, who can instead afford the financial sacrifice of government service. Stevenson was in a peculiarly good position to find men of this kind, because of his own background.

Appointing a man of probity to head a department does not necessarily mean that the department won't have any crooks in it. Crooks have a way of worming their way into the lower levels of bureaucracy and thieving there unnoticed until some event discovers them. The "pols," as politicians are called in Illinois, have scandalized the Stevenson administration, as we shall see in the next chapter. In fact scandal has touched one member of Stevenson's cabinet. But only one. And though directors of departments cannot do everything, honesty at the top is a long step in the right direction. If honesty is combined with administrative ability it can work wonders.

Let us study one example of how Stevenson picked his cabinet and what his cabinet has accomplished. The example: the Department of Public Welfare.

The Welfare Department is the State's biggest department. Over half the State's budget goes into the State's welfare institutions and public aid. The Welfare Department spends $121,-

000,000 every biennium. It employs 11,500 people—over a third
of all the state employees. There are over 50,000 people in public institutions run by the Welfare Department—correctional
institutions, children's hospitals, mental hospitals, schools for
the blind and deaf, and so on. To run all this, Stevenson wanted
to get either a businessman who'd been active in welfare work
or the administrative head of a big welfare agency. He sought
the advice of Dutch Smith, who was a member of the executive
committee of the Chicago Community Trust and vice-president
of the Community Fund of Chicago. Smith recommended Fred
Hoehler, executive director of the Community Fund. Stevenson
already knew Hoehler and immediately agreed.

Hoehler is a professional in welfare work, a recognized
authority in the field, president of the American Public Welfare Association and once president of the National Council
of Social Work. He had been in welfare work since 1926. He
had been welfare director and public safety director in Cincin-
nati. During and immediately after the war he had engaged in
relief and rehabilitation work in Europe and Africa for the
U.S. State Department and UNRRA. He had known Stevenson
in London. When Stevenson first asked Hoehler to become
Welfare Director, he declined, mainly because of his health.
Stevenson and his agents, including Smith, kept after him. Finally on a Sunday Stevenson telephoned Hoehler and asked him
to take the job for three months, just to get things started, and
to give Stevenson time to find a permanent Director. "And,"
Hoehler said recently, laughing, "I'm still here."

Other men joined Stevenson's administration on a temporary
basis and are still there.

Hoehler, a rather small friendly graying man of fifty-nine,
recalls, "When I took the job I wrote out my resignation and
left it undated and gave it to the Governor. He asked, 'What's
this?' I told him, 'I may get you all balled up with the poli-

ticians. If things get too hot you can put a date on this and accept it.' I told him, 'I know a lot about this welfare business and there are also a lot of things I don't know. What I don't know is how to handle these politicians. If I go in I want to build up a career service, make it attractive to good men, professionals in the field.' He told me that was what he wanted too and that I had a free hand."

Hoehler made a list of the jobs in his department that needed professional people—doctors, psychiatrists, social service workers, and others. He gave the list to Stevenson and told him, "These jobs are sacrosanct. They can't be filled by politicians." Stevenson agreed. "What's more," Hoehler recalls, "he made it stick. It hurt—lots of those jobs had been filled on a patronage basis in the past. It wasn't easy to change things. He had to resist all sorts of pressure. And he had to fight the battle over and over—those political fellows never give up. You say no to them today and tomorrow they're right back on your doorstep."

Traditionally, too, the superintendents of the several state institutions were political appointees. Before Hoehler took over, Stevenson appointed two superintendents on a political basis (Rednour, at Chester, whom we spent some time with in Chapter One, is one of these. Stevenson and Hoehler consider that he has nevertheless turned out well.) Since Hoehler took over, heads of institutions and heads of divisions within his department have been appointed on a nonpolitical basis.

Hoehler has said, "I found maybe forty or fifty payrollers in the department. I fired them all." He fired other political appointees. "I fired a Democratic state central committeeman. For good cause, too. You can imagine the heat that put on the Governor. But he made it stick. I fired a Chicago precinct captain and there was all kinds of hell to pay. It was a complicated affair—the man was a slave to his political sponsor. I'd discussed it with the man himself. His sponsor had got him into a job that he wasn't able to do. He wanted to get out from under the domination of his sponsor.

"Well, I fired him and his sponsor went to the Governor and accused the Governor of ruining the organization by firing good wheelhorses who rang doorbells. He even accused me of killing the man's father, said the father died of a heart attack because the man lost his job. The Governor told him that was nonsense, that I'd discussed it with the man before firing him and he was well prepared for it. The Governor also said, 'This man has told us he's a slave to his sponsor. I don't want anybody working for the State under those conditions.'" (One should know that in these circumstances a suspicion exists that the sponsor is exacting a salary kickback as tribute from the employee.) "We made the firing stick. Later on we gave the fellow a job he was fitted for and gave it to him independent of his sponsor. He was tickled to death. That's typical of the Governor—he said he thought the fellow didn't deserve to be out of a job just because of his sponsor. Stevenson never loses sight of the individual."

Awhile back Hoehler discovered that the inmates of a small state institution, some of whom were chronic alcoholics, were being allowed to buy drinks at taverns in town on credit. This is illegal. The superintendent had tried to stop it but had been frustrated by the county chairman and local politicians. Hoehler spoke to Governor Stevenson about it. Stevenson told him, "Go ahead—I don't care who gets hurt." State investigators, posing as institution inmates, obtained evidence which Hoehler took to the State's Attorney. The racket was broken up. Hoehler then met with town clergymen and businessmen, who previously had despised the institution, and persuaded them to develop a program of rehabilitating the inmates by finding jobs for them in the community.

When Stevenson was working on his first budget he called in

not only Hoehler but also the superintendents of all twenty-four Welfare Department institutions. "They were amazed," Hoehler says. "It was the first time in memory that the heads of institutions had been able to talk to the Governor himself about their needs."

A traditional source of graft in government is construction. Hoehler's department spends about $35,000,000 a biennium on construction. Hoehler discovered that although contracts had been awarded to the lowest bidder, as the law requires, a certain small group of contractors were the only bidders, and this raised in Hoehler's mind the question of whether there was collusion among them. After further inquiry he decided that construction costs the State five to ten per cent more than it should, largely because state specifications are "gold-plated"—high-priced items with a high markup are specified. Hoehler brought in outsiders to rewrite specifications, supervise the awarding of contracts, and do his purchasing.

State purchasing was for years a huge source of graft. State institutions paid top-grade prices for fourth-grade meat and fed it to the hapless inmates. They fed them rotten potatoes from bags marked "Grade A." Hoehler remembers a day shortly after he had taken office when, paying a visit to a state institution, he noticed that the place was full of apples. He recalls, "The superintendent had apples piled up one place, then another, apples all over, he had apples running out of his ears." Hoehler said nothing. Presently a truck drove up loaded with apples. The driver said to the gatekeeper, "Where you want these apples?"

The gatekeeper shrugged. "I don't care, put 'em anywhere you want to."

The superintendent, who with Hoehler happened to be close by, said, "Wait a minute—I don't think we need any more apples."

Hoehler said, "No, he doesn't need any apples, he's got lots of apples."

The truck driver said, "Oh, you'll take 'em."

The superintendent said, "Maybe you don't understand. I'm the new superintendent."

The trucker, who was from Chicago, said, "You'll learn. I been bringin' apples here for years. You'll learn."

The superintendent said, "Well, if I do I'll learn from this fella," and pointed to Hoehler.

The trucker said suspiciously, "Who're you?"

"I'm the new Director of the Department."

"Well, they told me to bring the apples here. They always tell me that. If I can't get rid of 'em anywhere else I dump 'em here and the fellow here knows how to get rid of 'em. I been doin' it for years."

Hoehler said, "Well, you won't leave this load here."

The trucker shrugged. "Okay, okay, I can always dump 'em at ———," and he named another state institution.

He drove away. Hoehler, indignant by this time, telephoned the superintendent of the other institution and told him not to accept the apples. The superintendent said, "Apples! I got lots of apples, apples everywhere. They must have been piling up for months."

Hoehler asked, "What do you do with them?"

"Well, we tried to make applesauce out of them but they were too rotten. So we been feeding them to the hogs."

"That," Hoehler says today, sighing, "is what you're up against." Apparently a Chicago fruit dealer with political connections had been dumping his surplus and overripe stock onto state institutions for years. To combat this sort of thing, which was extremely common, Hoehler reorganized his purchasing system.

He also makes a habit of dropping in on his institutions frequently and unexpectedly. Recently when he did so at one institution, he found the superintendent in the midst of a first-class row with one of the doctors. Flustered, the superintendent said, "This is quite a surprise, Director."

Hoehler said, "I know. It's a habit I've developed," and he sat down and, inviting the two men to continue their argument, helped settle it.

One should not get the impression that Hoehler has done nothing but play watchdog. True, a great deal of his time—and that of any conscientious administrator wallowing in the swamps of Illinois politics—is taken up with preventing deceit and outright theft. Nevertheless, Hoehler has initiated several important programs designed to improve the lot of the thousands of wards of the State and to promote research into the reasons why people become state wards.

Research ordinarily languishes in state Welfare Departments and in state institutions. Hoehler asked Dr. Percival Bailey, a world-famed neurosurgeon, to take over the Research Department. Bailey was reluctant. Hoehler argued that Bailey's prestige would attract research men of high caliber. He took Bailey to see the Governor. Stevenson has a way of drawing out anybody who visits him. Stevenson closed their interview by saying humbly, as he does at the end of almost every interview, "Thank you so much—you've been a tremendous help to me." Bailey left him almost starry-eyed. He took the job.

Hoehler, who has watched Stevenson charm many a man into undertaking public service against his will, has said, "The Governor has a way of making you *want* to help him out."

Bailey did persuade a number of outstanding research men to go to work for the State of Illinois, such as Dr. Harold Hemwich, a world-famed authority on nerve and brain metabolism. Dr. Hemwich is directing an ambitious research program in geriatrics, the branch of medicine dealing with old age and its diseases. This may result in a pioneer institute of geriatrics. Several other research programs have been launched. One is some basic research into the causes and treatments of mental illness. Another is research with special therapies for Mongoloid children and epileptics. Another is research into the use of an ultrasonic ray method of destroying brain tumors.

Dutch Smith has said, "You see how it works? You get a man like Adlai at the top and he can get a man like Hoehler to come in. Hoehler can get Dr. Bailey. And Dr. Bailey can get Dr. Hemwich. It works all down the line that way."

Hoehler has launched a program to improve the treatment of people "in the back wards," that is, the so-called incurables and seniles who, because their cases are thought to be hopeless, are neglected while the overworked staff deals with improvables. Thus the so-called incurables tend to get pushed further and further back, until they get lost in the dim vastness of the state hospitals. The result is still more overcrowding, a hopeless circular process. A program has been started to try special therapies—shock therapy, drug therapy, occupational therapy—on "back ward" patients.

This is one aspect of a broad policy of reducing the institutional population, a policy that flows directly from Stevenson's own concern: that welfare should not become a blind alley into which the unfortunate and handicapped are shunted, but rather, where possible, a thoroughfare to their rehabilitation.

Hoehler when he took office was shocked to find a large number of psychotic children scattered about the various institutions of the State. He talked to Stevenson. Stevenson has a deep interest in and sympathy for children. He agreed something had to be done, though there was no money to do it with. "So," said Hoehler, "I went to all the institutions, trying to find a place for the children, and the doctor at our Peoria Hospital said he had an old empty building that might be rehabilitated. We fixed it up and got the local community organizations to participate—women's clubs, social agencies, that sort of thing. They came out and decorated the building with Mother Goose rhymes, built a pond to sail boats on, tried to fix it up so these kids might have as near normal an existence as possible. Now we've got a unique institution—an institution for the care of psychotic children."

In all these programs, Hoehler has said, Stevenson has exhibited a knowledgeable interest. "He gives you backing, but it isn't blind backing. When you come to him with a new idea he wants to know all about it. Once he decides it's good, he'll back you all the way."

Stevenson has encouraged Hoehler to set up local clinics with a view to returning able patients to their home communities. This is a corollary of a bedrock idea that underlies a great many of Stevenson's measures: that the foundation of American society is the local community and that, concomitantly, the local community must accept responsibility.

Similarly, Stevenson has tried to force people able to pay for state institutional care to do so. He feels that it is only right and, furthermore, it would produce revenue and tend to reduce the institutional population. Stevenson feels that people ought not dump their problems onto the State. His is a moral position. It is also rather conservative. And it is extremely unpopular politically. He has persisted in it.

At the time that Hoehler took over the Illinois Welfare Department, professional people had almost despaired of it. Today it is considered one of the nation's best. Dr. Karl Menninger, the psychiatrist, said so. When Menninger was touring the state institutions Stevenson entertained him, Hoehler, and the superintendents of all the institutions at the Executive Mansion. "After dinner," Hoehler recalls, "we were supposed to talk over our problems—how to train personnel for the institutions, how to reduce the inmate population, what responsibilities local communities could assume—and the Governor whispered to me, 'You take over, I don't know anything about this.' But as soon as the discussion started he was in the thick of it. We talked till midnight. It was one of the best conferences I ever sat in on. Stevenson," he added, "is a great guy."

Other state departments and commissions offer less challenge than Welfare. Has Stevenson been able to attract other capable men?

He has reorganized and removed from politics the Commerce Commission, an extremely powerful and often venal body that regulates public utilities and common carriers. To head it he appointed Walter T. Fisher, a wealthy Winnetka man of broad experience in law, finance, and labor arbitration. (Awhile back Fisher told a friend who praised him for accepting public office, "Anybody has a right to indulge himself. Some people put their money in yachts, some people put it in stables. The Commerce Commission happens to be my luxury.")

As might be expected, the Illinois Parole Board is exposed to all sorts of pressures and temptations from the friends of gangsters who want out. To head his Parole Board Stevenson appointed Joseph D. Lohman, a University of Chicago criminologist with a national reputation.

Stevenson persuaded George W. Mitchell, a man of academic background, to take leave from a post as Federal Reserve economist and run the state Finance Department. When, after two years Mitchell begged leave to return to his private employment, Stevenson wouldn't let him go until he procured the services of Joseph Pois, an expert in government and business administrative organization who was at the time of his appointment a vice-president and member of the board of a steel-fabricating company in Chicago.

Stevenson appointed Henry F. Tenney, a wealthy lawyer from Winnetka long active in good works, to the Illinois Public Aid Commission. He appointed Maude Meyers, a career public servant, to the Civil Service Commission. To find a man for the job of State Purchasing Agent—a job sought eagerly by the pols, since it is the central buying agency for a multitude of state purchases—Stevenson sought the advice of many purchasing agents for private business as well as the heads of businesses; through General Robert E. Wood, chairman of the board of Sears, Roebuck (who, incidentally, had been a leading America First man), he found a man just retiring as purchasing agent for Sears, Carl Kresl.

The Taxpayers' Federation of Illinois said in March, 1952, "One of the greatest contributions Governor Stevenson has made to the cause of good government has been his ability to attract high-grade, competent men to state government service. In any barrel of apples there are going to be some that are rotten at the core although they look good on the outside. It's the rotten apples we hear about. The Taxpayers' Federation of Illinois believes the good apples should be given some attention too."

## STEVENSON AND THE LEGISLATURE

Stevenson's adventures in the brier patch called the Illinois General Assembly looked perilous from the beginning. He was a Democrat. The House was narrowly Democratic, the Senate Republican. Matters were, however, much worse than even that line-up indicates. The Illinois General Assembly contains a motley assortment of Solons. There are the downstate greeter types. There are the sturdy boys from Chicago's River Wards. There are the lobbyists' hirelings. There are the members of the West Side bloc, the political action arm of the Chicago Syndicate. And of course there are some decent lawgivers.

When an Illinois governor takes office, the Legislature is already in session—lying in ambush, waiting for him. The timing is dreadful—the new governor not only is obliged to appoint his cabinet officers and other administrative aides but he also must present to the Assembly his legislative program.

Stevenson presented to the Sixty-sixth Assembly in 1949 one of the most ambitious legislative programs of recent years. Too ambitious, many of his friends now feel. But he had the idea that he was obligated to make good on his campaign promises, and he was advised that he had to get everything done in the 1949 session—that in 1949 the legislators were awed by his overwhelming election victory but that by 1951 when next they met in biennial session they would have his number, he would have made mistakes, and his prestige would have waned.

And so he went before the General Assembly and asked for, among other things, state aid to local government, a constitutional convention to write a new constitution for Illinois, increase in salaries for state officers and employees, strengthening of Civil Service, increased school aid, integration of services in the Departments of Public Welfare and Labor, increased workmen's compensation and unemployment compensation, a state FEPC, highway reconstruction and improvement (requiring a raise in the gas tax from three to five cents), extension of Civil Service to the Department of Mines and Minerals and revision of the mining laws, taking the Conservation Department and the State Police out of politics, lengthened terms and increased compensation for the Illinois Commerce Commission, and a series of laws advocated by the Chicago Crime Commission to combat organized crime.

Of this program he succeeded in getting through the 1949 Legislature the following measures: the removal of the State Police from politics, increased workmen's compensation, increased school aid, reorganization of the Department of Mines and Minerals, increased pay for state officers and employees, lengthened terms and increased salaries for the Illinois Commerce Commission members, and strengthened Civil Service.

He failed to get the constitutional convention, though he accepted a Republican alternative, the Gateway Amendment, which relaxed to a considerable extent the extremely restrictive amending procedure in Illinois. FEPC failed in both 1949 and 1951. The increase in the gas tax also failed in 1949.

The hotel lobbies, Statehouse anterooms, chambers of the Legislature, and Governor's office during any session of the Legislature are chaotic. In 1949 they were sometimes nearly hysterical. In addition to the customary hordes of office-seekers, fixers, legislators, lobbyists, and connivers, large numbers of uplifters and planners descended on Springfield.

Reform was in the air and so was opposition to reform. Lou Kohn was on hand in the anteroom of the Governor's office in the Statehouse, acting as one of Stevenson's administrative aides, trying to be everywhere at one time, serving, as he was fond of saying, as the Governor's lobbyist. The anteroom was always jammed with people. They besieged the new Governor who had not yet learned to turn them away. While dealing with them Stevenson tried to listen through a monitoring system to debate in the legislative chambers.

One of the architects of Stevenson's legislative program was Walter Schaefer, the Northwestern law professor. Before any bill can be introduced, a tremendous amount of legal spadework must be done. Schaefer saw that it got done. "He was a new type for those boys down there," one man has said, "a quiet professor."

Schaefer was, in fact, too quiet. The man upon whom devolved the onerous task of getting down in the mud and wrestling with the legislators was Jim Mulroy. He it was who drank with the Solons in the hotel rooms, who arranged the deals and did the horse-trading. This is a dirty job. Some of the dirt, as we shall see, rubbed off on Jim Mulroy.

That '49 Legislature was Stevenson's baptism in rough-and-tumble politics. It shocked and dismayed him. Some people are inclined to think that when he says, as he often does, that he was surprised by the shenanigans of the legislators he is dissembling, is only playing a favorite role, that of political amateur. There is, however, every reason to believe that his shock was genuine. He had known, of course, much about what are often called the realities of politics. But there are some things you can't really know until they've happened to you. Stevenson was, for example, genuinely startled to discover that Republican legislators, in order to embarrass him politically, voted against measures he proposed even though they themselves under the previous Republican administration had favored them. He was no doubt equally surprised that it was the *Tribune* that rescued his budget in the course of an extremely complicated deal.

Several times during the 1949 Legislature Stevenson slipped away from Springfield to spend week ends in Lake Forest with his friends. He kept telling them, "I'm rattled." He felt hemmed in by powerful forces. Dutch Smith recalls, "This was a bunch of amateurs from the beginning. When Adlai first took the job he kept saying, 'This is terrible, I don't know where to begin, all these appointments to make and laws to propose.' I remember somebody kept after him to give some criminal or other a parole. The man was from one of the River Wards, as I recall, and they kept telling Adlai if he didn't parole him he'd never carry that ward again. Well, he didn't parole him."

Once, the Smiths remember, "he was very discouraged." He was fighting desperately to get through the Legislature a resolution calling for a constitutional convention. As a lawyer he felt—and indeed rightly: the Illinois constitution was adopted in 1870 and is sadly out of date—that a new constitution was of first importance if Illinois ever was to be lifted out of the mud. Strong opposition had developed, however. And some of it was rather unexpected: the members of the Chicago West Side bloc, for example, opposed it. But presently their purpose became clear. They came to Stevenson and offered him a deal: if he would abandon his support of the Chicago Crime Commission bills that would make life harder for hoodlums, they in turn would muster enough votes to pass "Con-Con," as the resolution for a constitutional convention was called. Stevenson was appalled. That anything so fundamentally vital as the State's organic act should depend upon the favor of the West Side bloc shocked him. He refused the deal.

And now in Lake Forest, Mrs. Smith recalls, "He sat down at the edge of the lake and just stared at it. I asked him what was the matter. He said, 'I'm discouraged. I sometimes wonder if I can do it if I keep turning down deals. Now I'll probably lose both the Crime bills *and* Con-Con. How am I going to do anything useful? Maybe it'd be better to go ahead and make deals like that.' " But he didn't mean it. He made no deal. As a result he did lose both Con-Con and the Crime bills. But he salvaged something: when Con-Con was beaten, he immediately shifted his support to the Gateway Amendment, and this passed. Subsequently, in the 1951 Legislature, he got the most important of the Crime bills passed.

In Illinois the legislative session must for all practical purposes end on June 30. The Legislature passes most of its bills in the last few days of the session. This means that the Governor can veto them and the Legislature has no chance to override his veto.

As the 1949 Legislature drew to a close it became clear that Stevenson intended to veto a large number of bills it was going to pass. So the Republican leader in the Senate in order to embarrass Stevenson moved to adjourn the Senate until July 18 instead of adjourning *sine die* as is customary.

Stevenson, after long consideration, decided to prorogue the Legislature—that is, end its session by executive order, a measure with origins in early English constitutional history and one not attempted in a regular session of the Illinois Legislature since the 1890's. The tactics that had to be employed were extremely intricate. Schaefer acted as field general. A series of resolutions had to be passed by the two houses to establish a condition of disagreement on adjournment between them. Great care had to be taken to prevent the Republican opposition from apprehending the executive plot. On the night of June 30 the Legislature, as is usual, stopped the clock to stay in session and wind up its business. These last-night sessions are always hectic. A cynical observer once said, "If you ever want to buy a legislator wait till the last night—you can buy one for five dollars." Schaefer and other Stevenson agents were running back and forth between the chambers and the Governor's office.

Their labors succeeded. Stevenson prorogued the Legislature at 5:35 A.M. by proclamation in both houses. One of his aides recalls, "I'll never forget the look on the Republican leader's face in the Senate when the Lieutenant Governor read the proclamation. He jumped to his feet and started hollering and he was still hollering when the gavel banged and it was all over."

Interestingly enough Stevenson's program fared better in the 1951 Legislature than in the 1949, although by 1951 *both* houses were Republican. There were many reasons for this peculiar success. Most are of merely local interest. Of more importance is this: by 1951 Stevenson had learned that certain legislators with whom he disagreed didn't have horns, and they had learned that he was not primarily interested in saying out loud that they did have.

Senator Douglas, who has an academic background, once said that he had entered the Chicago City Council armed with the satisfying knowledge that some of his fellow aldermen had never got beyond the eighth grade, but had discovered that they could nevertheless beat his head bloody. Maybe they weren't educated, but they were smart, and no Ph.D. withstood them. Douglas dates his political education from this salutary if sanguinary postgraduate course. Stevenson never has made any such public declaration but it is not unlikely that he would subscribe to it.

By 1951 Stevenson had demonstrated that his attitude toward the Legislature, in public at least, was conciliatory. In reporting to the people on the deeds and misdeeds of the 1949 Legislature he had not castigated the Legislature as "the worst." He had in fact done remarkably little name-calling. His attitude toward the Legislature, as toward everyone else, was and has remained reasonable, persuasive, conciliatory—never dogmatic, stubborn, vindictive. He had cozened some of the legislators and bewitched others. And all this bore fruit.

Moreover, by 1951, his prestige had increased considerably, not declined as predicted. The people held him in high esteem. He operated quietly and without fireworks but people seemed to feel he was giving them good government. Legislators hesitate to attack a man holding that position.

Finally, by 1951, Stevenson had established firmer political control in his own party. Civic groups and newspapers respected and supported his legislative program. He had begun to realize that he was the best asset the Democratic Party had in Illinois. So he started using his power, as we shall see.

And he had developed his own skill in personally obtaining agreement on bills he wanted passed. Here is an example of how he operates: Illinois highways, like the highways of other states, had gone to pieces during the war. Stevenson proposed legislation in 1951, as he had in 1949, to increase the gasoline tax and to force trucks to bear more of the cost of building and maintaining the highways. The truck lobbyists descended on Springfield with their pockets stuffed with money. Stevenson's proposals would cost them $28,000,000 a year. Stevenson took his fight to the people by radio and through the newspapers. As usual, he eschewed invective for a simple, almost naïve statement that what he wanted was only right and he couldn't see why anybody was objecting. Since this happened to be true, it worked. Even Republican newspapers backed him.

And at the same time, Stevenson was active behind the scenes. His press secretary, Bill Flanagan, was feeding information to the newspapers. His executive secretary, Mulroy, buttonholed members of the House; another aide, Dick Nelson, buttonholed Senators. They were applying political pressure.

The lobbyists tried a new tactic. They reopened an old sore: the Chicago-downstate rivalry. They pulled into the fight local politicians who wanted the extra revenue for township roads, motor clubs from Chicago who wanted it for arterial highways, and special interests of all kinds. Half the problems of state government got entangled in the brawl such as the old controversy about consolidation of rural school districts. It was the truckers' hope, of course, that a confused and hopeless stalemate would result.

At a critical point Stevenson called the various antagonists together for a meeting at the Executive Mansion. He sat them down around his desk and told them that they had to compose their differences if anything at all was to be accomplished. He kept them there until, about 3:00 A.M., they reached a compromise. The bills passed. Men who have watched him operate at such meetings say his talent for personal negotiation is unsurpassed. It is a talent developed at preliminary sessions of the United Nations.

Stevenson has used his veto power extensively. One of his administrative assistants, Carl McGowan, a young lawyer who helps prepare his veto messages, has said, "I think I could write a history of the Stevenson administration and an exposition of his philosophy of government from the vetoes alone. Anybody can make a speech. But a veto represents the Governor's final decision. It is not just talk." A veto is by definition a negative act but it often is a very positive and very difficult act to perform.

Vetoes are prepared under great pressure. As has been said, the Legislature customarily dumps five or six hundred bills on the Governor's desk at the end of its session. He has ten days in which to veto them. The Attorney General passes on their constitutionality, then sends them on to Stevenson's staff. By this time Stevenson, having followed the bills through the Legislature, usually knows which ones he is going to veto. Sometimes Stevenson starts writing his veto messages from scratch. More commonly some member of his staff prepares a draft—usually McGowan or Blair nowadays, Schaefer or Day formerly. The draft goes to Stevenson and he works it over.

"What comes out is his own," McGowan has said. This is true. Stevenson likes to write and he writes well. His aides think he spends too much time writing, time he should be devoting to what they consider his greatest talent, speaking to the people. Over the last twenty years his speeches, his veto messages, and his published writings all have a distinctive touch, which is his own.

Stevenson has vetoed about ten per cent of the bills passed by the Legislature. He probably would have vetoed more if he had had an adequate legal staff to help. His vetoes are closely reasoned and tightly written. Some of them required considerable political courage.

He vetoed the so-called Broyles Bill which had the announced purpose of searching out subversive activities by requiring loyalty oaths of teachers and state officials—and he vetoed it in 1951, at a time when Senator McCarthy was going great guns. In doing so Stevenson wrote:

The stated purpose of this bill is to combat the menace of world Communism. That the Communist Party—and all it stands for—is a danger to our Republic, as real as it is sinister, is clear to all who have the slightest understanding of our democracy. No one attached to the principles of our society will debate this premise or quarrel with the objectives of this bill.

Agreed upon ends, our concern is with means. It is in the choice of methods to deal with recognized problems that we Americans, in and out of public life, so often develop differences of opinion. Our freedom to do so is a great source of strength and if not impaired by mistakes of our own, will contribute greatly to the ultimate confusion of the enemies of freedom.

The issue with respect to means raised by this bill has two aspects. One is the question of the need for it in relation to existing weapons for the control of subversives. The other is whether this addition to our arsenal may not be a two-edged sword, more dangerous to ourselves than to our foes.

Were the latter alone involved, I should hesitate to impose my judgment upon that of the majority of the General Assembly. But it is precisely because the evil at hand has long since been identified and provided against that we here in Illinois need not now do something bad just for the sake of doing something.

The bill, he said, was "wholly unnecessary"—Federal antisubversive law and policing was adequate and, moreover, Illinois had had an antisubversive law of its own since 1919; indeed, a Maryland law upon which the Broyles Bill was patterned was itself enacted in an effort to make Maryland's sedition laws as comprehensive as Illinois'. Not only was there no need for the Broyles Bill, but Stevenson considered its enforcement provisions highly objectionable, since they tended toward the dangerous "perpetuation of rumors and hearsay." As to the loyalty oath provisions, Stevenson wrote:

Does anyone seriously think that a real traitor will hesitate to sign a loyalty oath? Of course not. Really dangerous subversives and saboteurs will be caught by careful, constant, professional investigation, not by pieces of paper.

The whole notion of loyalty inquisitions is a natural characteristic of the police state, not of democracy. Knowing his rule rests upon compulsion rather than consent, the dictator must always assume the disloyalty, not of a few but of many, and guard against it by continual inquisition and "liquidation" of the unreliable. The history of Soviet Russia is a modern example of this ancient practice. The democratic state, on the other hand, is based on the consent of its members. The vast majority of our people are intensely loyal, as they have amply demonstrated. To question, even by implication, the loyalty and devotion of a large group of citizens is to create an atmosphere of suspicion and distrust which is neither justified, healthy nor consistent with our traditions.

Legislation of this type, in Illinois and elsewhere, is the direct result of the menacing gains of Communism in Europe and Asia. But it would be unrealistic, if not naïve, to assume that such legislation would be effective in combating Communist treachery in America. Such state laws have nowhere uncovered a single case of subversive disloyalty.

Basically, the effect of this legislation, then, will be less the detection of subversives and more the intimidation of honest citizens. But we cannot suppress thought and expression and preserve the freedoms guaranteed by the Bill of Rights. This is our dilemma. In time of danger we seek to protect ourselves from sedition, but in doing so we imperil the very freedoms we seek to protect, just as we did in the evil atmosphere of the alien and sedition laws of John Adams' administration and just as Britain did during the Napoleonic era. To resolve the dilemma we will all agree that in the last analysis the Republic must be protected at all costs, or there will be no freedoms to preserve or even regain. But if better means of protection already exist, then surely we should not further imperil the strength of freedom in search of illusory safety.

We must fight traitors with laws. We already have the laws. We must fight falsehood and evil ideas with truth and better ideas. We have them in plenty. But we must not confuse the two. Laws infringing our rights and intimidating unoffending persons without enlarging our security will neither catch subversives nor win converts to our better ideas. And in the long run evil ideas can be counteracted and conquered not by laws but only by better ideas.

Finally, the states are not, in my judgment, equipped to deal with the threat of the world Communist movement which inspired this bill. Communism threatens us because it threatens world peace. The great problems with which Communism confronts us are problems of foreign relations and national defense. Our Constitution wisely leaves the solution of such matters to the national government.

In conclusion, while I respect the motives and patriotism of the proponents of this bill, I think there is in it more of danger to the liberties we seek to protect than of security for the Republic. It reverses our traditional concept of justice by placing upon the accused the burden of proving himself innocent. It makes felons of persons who may be guilty more of bad judgment than of anything else. It jeopardizes the freedom of sincere and honest citizens in an attempt to catch and punish subversives. It is unnecessary and redundant.

I know full well that this veto will be distorted and misunderstood, even as telling the truth of what I knew about the reputation of Alger Hiss was distorted and misunderstood. I know that to veto this bill in this period of grave anxiety will be unpopular with many. But I must, in good conscience, protest against any unnecessary suppression of our ancient rights as free men. Moreover, we will win the contest of ideas that afflicts the world not by suppressing these rights, but by their triumph. We must not burn down the house to kill the rats.

Stevenson vetoed dozens of pork-barrel bills. Among these are bills appropriating money to construct certain roads or bridges.

They are the equivalent of the notorious Rivers and Harbors Bill that Congress passes. They benefit nobody but the constituents of the Solon who introduces them. To veto them often costs a governor the legislator's support.

He vetoed many of the so-called Christmas Tree Bills, appropriating funds for various private groups, such as specific veterans' organizations.

Such appropriations are traditional in Illinois politics; it is an act of political courage to kill them. Stevenson did so in order to keep his budget in balance. He had presented carefully worked out budgets that were in what he called "precarious balance." The Legislature had destroyed the balance by refusing to vote taxes to raise the additional revenues he asked for but at the same time increasing the bills appropriating funds. The last session cut $300,000 from his budget and increased his appropriations by $50,000,000. Such fiscal irresponsibility horrifies Stevenson.

Stevenson has worked into even so unlikely a spot as his veto messages some of his wit, as when he vetoed the Cat Bill:

To the Honorable, the Members of the Senate of the Sixty-sixth General Assembly:

I herewith return, without my approval, Senate Bill No. 93 entitled "An Act to Provide Protection to Insectivorous Birds by Restraining Cats." This is the so-called "Cat Bill." I veto and withhold my approval from this bill for the following reasons:

It would impose fines on owners or keepers who permitted their cats to run at large off their premises. It would permit any person to capture, or call upon the police to pick up and imprison, cats at large. It would permit the use of traps. The bill would have state-wide application—on farms, in villages, and in metropolitan centers.

This legislation has been introduced in the past several sessions of the Legislature, and it has, over the years, been the source of much comment—not all of which has been in a serious vein. It may be that the General Assembly has now seen fit to refer it to one who can view it with a fresh outlook. Whatever the reasons for passage at this session, I cannot believe there is a widespread public demand for this law or that it could, as a practical matter, be enforced.

Furthermore, I cannot agree that it should be the declared public policy of Illinois that a cat visiting a neighbor's yard or crossing the highway is a public nuisance. It is in the nature of cats to do a certain amount of unescorted roaming. Many live with their owners in apartments or other restricted premises, and I doubt if we want to make their every brief foray an opportunity for a small game hunt by zealous citizens—with traps or otherwise. I am afraid this bill could only create discord, recrimination and enmity. Also consider the owner's dilemma: To escort a cat abroad on a leash is against the nature of the cat, and to permit it to venture forth for exercise unattended into a night of new dangers is against the nature of the owner. Moreover, cats perform useful service, particularly in rural areas, in combatting rodents—work they necessarily perform alone and without regard for property lines.

We are all interested in protecting certain varieties of birds. That cats destroy some birds, I well know, but I believe this legislation would further but little the worthy cause to which its proponents give such unselfish effort. The problem of the cat versus bird is as old as time. If we attempt to resolve it by legislation who knows but what we may be called upon to take sides as well in the age-old problems of dog versus cat, bird versus bird, or even bird versus worm. In my opinion, the State of Illinois and its local governing bodies already have enough to do without trying to control feline delinquency.

For these reasons, and not because I love birds the less or cats the more, I veto and withhold my approval from Senate Bill No. 93.

Respectfully,

ADLAI E. STEVENSON, *Governor*

Stevenson vetoed an extremely complex bill changing the law of joint right and obligations. After fighting his way through the legal jungle of its meaning he concluded:

The basic difficulty stems, I repeat, from the failure to deal with the Act as an entirety rather than on this piecemeal basis. The next session of the Legislature can address itself to a more inclusive revision of the law and with, I hope, some prior measure of agreement among the bar, although—lawyers being what they are—this last may be an exercise in self-delusion on my part. Meanwhile, it will not be too serious if practices dating from the time of Henry VIII survive another two years.

## STEVENSON AND THE PEOPLE

Stevenson took office determined to work at the job of being Governor. He badly wanted to avoid a criticism often made of his predecessor, Governor Green: that he made too many public appearances. People thought Green spent more time junketing than governing.

Stevenson soon discovered, however, that it was impossible to resist the demands of people in Illinois who want to see their Governor. Little by little he relaxed his schedule, permitting his aides to commit him to more and more public appearances, until today he probably spends as much or even more time that way than Green did.

This does not necessarily mean, however, that the time so spent is wasted. It is possible for a governor or mayor to make public appearances utterly devoid of meaning. He can show up to dedicate a courthouse, or to cut a ribbon, or to unveil a monument, and in doing so he needs do nothing more. Stevenson does more. He makes speeches, and speeches that are not empty. As we saw in Chapter One, he used a small-town Rotary's twenty-fifth anniversary as an occasion to elucidate state fiscal affairs. Stevenson nearly always uses these occasions to say something to the people that he thinks is worth saying.

Through all his speeches run certain themes. They are ideas that are basic in his political thought and his character. He feels deeply that they are extremely important. He has an earnestness of manner and a simple directness of attack that command respect. People listen to him.

There is nothing very novel about these ideas of his. Their novelty lies in the fact that he really believes them and can convince others that he does.

He believes that people ought to pay attention to government. This is to him a moral question—the word "ought" is used advisedly. He likes to remind an audience, "You are citizens first, veterans second."

Yet somehow he never seems schoolmasterish, never seems to chide. Instead, he almost apologetically tells people that he wishes they would listen to him for a little while as he tries to explain something about "your government." He is never authoritarian or dogmatic in tone. Rather, he persuades—he often asks, "Doesn't it boil down to this?" His Welfare Director, Hoehler, has said, "He has an amazing ability to sell a program to the people."

Government interests Stevenson deeply. His education enables him to view it with a detachment rare in politicians. He is able to communicate some of this interest to his hearers.

He often speaks of "states' rights and states' wrongs." He fears that the state, which he conceives as a fulcrum balancing a teeter-totter at one end of which sits the Federal Government and the other end of which sits the local community, is neglected by citizens. He feels that people pay too much attention to national and local affairs, too little to state affairs. He feels that a concentration of Federal power will result, and this he dreads in an almost Jeffersonian way. Constantly he reminds people that it is the state and the local community that support the schools, maintain the streets, and perform hundreds of other functions that people take for granted.

He thinks a way must be found of "glamourizing" state government. To this task he addresses himself, in speaking to groups and in radio and television broadcasts to the public at large. He delivers six-months reports to the people by radio. Every month he puts on a half-hour Sunday afternoon television show, discussing with one of his cabinet members some aspect of Illinois government. All this constitutes a sort of continuing public seminar in political science.

A concomitant basic theme of his is the importance and the responsibility of the individual. He never emphasizes the aspect of importance to the neglect of the aspect of responsibility. (Thus, he thinks it "right" that the state should care for an insane person; but he thinks it equally "right" that that person's relatives should pay part of the cost of the care if they are able; and he does not hesitate to say so.)

One gets the impression reading large quantities of his speeches that their major themes all have a common and almost old-fashioned moral base, the good-and-evil dichotomy. It comes out in various ways—Efficient Government vs. Payrolling, Tight Budgeting vs. Political Spending, the Quality of Education vs. Spending School Money, Enforcement of Gambling Laws vs. Slot Machines in Private Clubs, Integration of Services vs. Duplicative Waste, Effective Care for Unfortunates vs. Doles.

He enjoys carrying a fight to an audience. He does it not belligerently but quietly, in a way that startles but does not antagonize his hearers. Once he addressed the State Convention of the American Legion on slot machines in Legion posts. (He pointed out the inconsistency of citizens who deplore organized gambling but play slot machines in their own clubs.) Once, speaking at a country club where it was all too apparent that the slot machine had been hidden in anticipation of his arrival, he told his hearers something that only a handful of them knew: that the last time he had visited the club a child had handed him a card to autograph and, turning it over, he saw that it bore a statement worded so that, when he had added his signature, it would read in effect:

The slot machines in this club are for members only and meet with my approval.

ADLAI E. STEVENSON

He chid the members gently.

Stevenson, who as we have seen was once a speech-writer himself, employs no speech-writer in the ordinary sense. Don Hyndman, a former newspaperman who helped Governor Green prepare speeches, performs the same chore for Stevenson. Customarily Stevenson tells Hyndman where he is to speak and what, in general, he wants to talk about. Hyndman gets up a rough draft. Stevenson then reworks it himself. On some speeches Carl McGowan may do the preliminary draft. In any case Stevenson rewrites extensively. Sometimes he even starts from scratch. His old files contain many holographic manuscripts, written in his hand on a lawyer's pad of ruled yellow paper. As his speech-making schedule became heavier he was obliged to delegate much of this rough drafting to Hyndman.

Like McGowan, Hyndman thinks Stevenson enjoys writing and would prefer to write all his own speeches if time permitted. The changes Stevenson makes in manuscripts are likely to range all the way from marking a letter upper case to cutting and sharpening paragraphs to recasting ideas completely. Like many professional writers, he is never satisfied with his product and keeps making changes right up to the last minute: the galley proofs of his message to the Sixty-seventh General Assembly contain heavy revision, and he sometimes makes changes in mimeographed speech texts released to the newspapers.

Stevenson has a felicity of expression rare in public men. He has a considerable respect for and knowledge of the English language. Sometimes he uses the same idea over and over in varying contexts. With him this is not poverty but economy. It is the same as his penchant for wearing old clothes. They are old but they are good and it would be wrong, wicked even, to discard them while they still were useful.

His advisers have encouraged him to speak more often extemporaneously. He does extemporize a great deal but he feels uncomfortable if he rises before an audience without a text of some sort.

He is a good speaker. He is at his best in a personal appearance. His personality comes through less clearly on radio but it does come through. On television, he seems to have himself notably under control.

The humor in his speeches is of two kinds, both effective: crowd-warming jokes and integral wit tightly related to the subject at hand. Much of it is at his own expense. He often assumes the role of an ineffectual hand-wringing lamb lost among wolves. His wit is dry. It works.

Stevenson has learned to address a gathering of farmers at a corn festival with the same aplomb that he brings to a meeting of the Council on Foreign Relations. Many times he has made four or five speeches in a single day. Once he addressed the State Convention of the American Legion in the afternoon and introduced Trygve Lie at the annual dinner of the United Nations Association of Greater Chicago that night. He does not hesitate to quote Sumner Slichter, the economist, while addressing a Jackson Day dinner attended largely by precinct doorbell-ringers.

Unlike many public officials, he has not developed a deepseated cynicism about the public intelligence. Many public officials conclude that people are unable to judge their public officials, that the electorate is not very bright. Considerable evidence exists to support this view but it is a view ultimately fatal to a public official, for he cannot conceal it. Stevenson started out with a deep respect for public opinion. He appears still to have it. He never talks down to an audience. He never feels relieved of an obligation to account to the people. This, at bottom, probably explains the great respect so many people have for him. The thing one hears said about him most commonly is, "He's obviously honest and sincere." This will carry a man a long way in American public life.

### STEVENSON AND THE POLS

"The pols," as politicians are called in Illinois, can make or break a public man, however good his intentions. As Mayor Kennelly of Chicago has so ably demonstrated, honesty is not enough. Mayor Kennelly has been scrupulously honest. He has been at great pains to divorce himself from the machine. This has left the machine free to do as it pleased. While Kennelly has been out cutting ribbons, the host of little crooks in Chicago government have stolen merrily along. Mayor Ed Kelly, a master politician, once said, "If you don't run the machine it will run you." In a memorial broadcast after Kelly's death in 1950, Stevenson said the same thing another way: "[Kelly] will be studied by students of politics as a leader who was never afraid to lead." Kennelly has failed to lead, he has failed to run the machine. In the American system, the little crooks that creep into the darker recesses of government and the powerful interests that press upon its total structure can undo all good intentions. Many a reform administration has foundered because the reformer in charge didn't understand political power. Stevenson understands political power.

Some of Stevenson's friends have criticized him for "playing ball" with the machine. They do not understand, as he does, that when decent people abstain from political leadership, the resulting vacuum is always filled by somebody else, and "somebody else" is likely to be in Chicago the petty crooks and the Syndicate.

Stevenson is still fond of saying, four years after his campaign for Governor, that he is an "amateur" at politics. This is disingenuous. He says the Cook County organization "adopted" him. There is truth in this. But it does not mean the machine runs him. In matters that affect him, he runs the machine.

He is able to do so first because of the respect, already mentioned, that he commands among the public at large. This is by no means enough, though it is a tremendous asset, since politicians hesitate to attack a man in that position.

More important, he does so because he has recognized his own power as the greatest asset the Democrats of Illinois possess. He would deny this, since it seems to imply that he is a dictator and any suggestion of authoritarianism is deeply abhorrent to him. Nevertheless, there is considerable evidence that it is true.

The clearest evidence that he is a powerful politician in the Illinois Democratic Party came early this year. The Cook County Committee met to make up its slate of candidates. The incumbent Cook County State's Attorney, John S. Boyle, wanted to run for re-election. The Committee seemed to be about to accept him, despite the fact that Boyle had been widely criticized for the way he had handled a race riot in Cicero, a murder committed by one of his own policemen, several cases involving Chicago Syndicate gamblers and sluggers, and other matters. Suddenly Stevenson, who, it had been assumed, would run for re-election as Governor, announced that he didn't know whether he'd be a candidate again or not. Stevenson recently had had a lot to say about organized gambling and about law enforcement by local officials. His press secretary, Flanagan, explained that Stevenson was concerned that the Cook County Committee slate a "first-rate fearless" man for State's Attorney who "could make some real progress" in cleaning up crime in Cook County. For several days the outcome was in doubt. Finally the County Committee dumped Boyle and nominated another man. Stevenson thereupon announced that he himself would run for re-election as Governor. (Boyle subsequently ran in the primary against the organization man and was badly beaten. Stevenson spoke in behalf of the organization man.)

Stevenson has denied this whole story, emphasizing that he never has dictated to any county committee. The story is nonetheless true. Stevenson, in effect, forced the Committee to drop a man he considered unsuitable by withholding himself from the Party, which needs him to carry the State this year.

In announcing his candidacy for re-election Stevenson said, "I invite the Republican Party to nominate the best man it can find. It is of little importance whether the next Governor of Illinois is named Adlai Stevenson; but it is of the highest importance that he finish what we have started. No matter then who loses, the people will win. That is the kind of an election Illinois needs and deserves. I am gladly and proudly ready to take part in it."

# CHAPTER V

# Stevenson Today

A TRAVELER arriving in Springfield receives an impression of a rather pleasant flat Midwestern town set down on the Illinois prairie, its brick streets lined with big old houses and trees right down to the edge of the business district. Presently the traveler notes with a twinge of suspicion that Springfield's chief export seems to be memories of Abraham Lincoln—the largest hotel is named for Abraham Lincoln, signs on every street corner point the ways to Lincoln's home and Lincoln's tomb, Lincoln's statue stands on the Statehouse steps and his face adorns the doors of taxicabs. And then the traveler sees in the hotel lobbies and the dingy barrooms the habitants—stringy county chairmen, swarthy Chicagoans in wide-brimmed Stetsons, beefy men sporting gaudy neckties emblazoned "Stratton for Governor," lady office-holders arguing noisily in a tavern about the 1948 Stevenson-Green campaign, the whole horde of job-holders and job-seekers, public officials and candidates, lobbyists and connivers and fixers, all with their eyes on the enormous domed Statehouse that dominates the town; and the impression is inescapable that Springfield is a rather grubby town.

It is therefore a pleasant relief to visit the Executive Mansion. Completed in 1856, it stands a couple of blocks from the center of town but it seems much farther removed than that. The

Mansion is a large somewhat ungainly structure of brick painted white. It sits atop a grassy knoll. No fence surrounds the block on which it stands. The walls of the Mansion have many high narrow windows, the roof has many gables. There is something vaguely Southern about the Mansion, outside and inside.

The Mansion looks clean. The interior walls are white or tinted in cool pale colors. The place looks swept-out.

One enters on the ground floor, a floor usually described, though misleadingly, as a basement. It is merely an old-fashioned first floor that sits right on the ground. The front door is kept locked. A State Policeman guards it. Inside, off a dark corridor to the right are the offices of two of Governor Stevenson's administrative assistants and, to the left, his private secretary's office and his own office, all rather small and unpretentious.

It is rather unusual to find more than two or three visitors here. The atmosphere is quiet and easygoing. There are the chatter of a single typewriter, a burst of laughter from two of Stevenson's young assistants chatting in an office, the padding of a dog's feet on the corridor floor.

Stevenson's office is a long narrow low-ceilinged room. The lighting is subdued, the carpeting thick. Against the walls stand a few chairs and two couches upholstered in soft green leather. In the center of the room a long directors' table runs up to form a T with Stevenson's desk. There is a window behind his desk. On the desk are a pile of letters and clippings and memoranda, two ashtrays, a telephone, and, beneath a sheet of glass, a road map of Illinois and a map showing Illinois' senatorial districts. Behind his swivel chair stand the flags of Illinois and the United States. His briefcases are piled on the radiator.

Flanking the window are bookcases containing a curious assortment of books—copies of the *Political Science Quarterly*, a life of Herbert Hoover, the state papers of Franklin D. Roosevelt, a history of the Kentucky Derby, an Illinois state guide, *Who's Who in America,* a manual called *The Police and Minority Groups* written by the chairman of the Illinois Parole Board, Joseph D. Lohman, the autobiography of Will Rogers, a book on General Erwin Rommel, sets of the laws of Illinois and opinions of the Attorney General and an *Illinois Blue Book,* plus a considerable number of books on special phases of politics or sociology published by university presses. On the bookcases too stand a bust of Lincoln, a small Liberty Bell, photographs of Stevenson's sons and a picture of President Truman autographed, "My best to a great governor, Adlai E. Stevenson, from his good friend, Harry Truman."

On the office walls are paintings of Stevenson's grandfather, the Vice-President, and of his father, together with the facsimile Lincoln autobiography and an old lithograph.

The Mansion has twenty-eight rooms. On the second floor are drawing rooms, a music room, the state dining room, a smaller dining room, and a pleasant tile-floored sun porch that Stevenson has made into a library. (He has sought to persuade people to donate books to a permanent Mansion library in honor of the memory of the author, Lloyd Lewis, a neighbor and friend of his. He thinks the Mansion ought to have a decent library.)

The rooms are spacious, the ceilings high, the chandeliers crystal, the period-style furniture old and a trifle faded but good. Here too are family pictures—pictures of ancestors, of Stevenson's boys, of Stevenson in hunting clothes shooting geese with the Director of Conservation. A circular staircase leads to the bedrooms on the top floor. The subdued mutter of a typewriter on the ground floor can be heard even there.

Stevenson has an office in the Statehouse, a few blocks away, but he rarely uses it. Too many people keep dropping in, he can't get any work done there. It is a small office with a tremendous anteroom. The anteroom is, like everything else in the Statehouse, adorned with heavy carved walnut woodwork and gilded ornamental plasterwork, and on the high arched ceiling is what looks to be a fresco of cherubs. Stevenson had the anteroom redecorated last year. But he had the walls painted only up to the ornamental plasterwork—too expensive to have that done.

### STEVENSON'S DAY

Stevenson of course sleeps at the Mansion. He begins an ordinary day with breakfast at eight-thirty. Usually he has a guest at breakfast to discuss business, frequently one of his cabinet members. He is at his desk at nine. By that time his appointment secretary, Bill Blair, is on hand, having read the morning papers. Blair lives in the Mansion too, its only other occupant. Blair tells him the news and goes over his day's schedule with him.

If Stevenson has just returned from a trip he is likely to keep the day free to clear his desk of accumulated work. Otherwise he has appointments all day, often a dozen or more. They are supposed to last a half-hour on an average but frequently Stevenson becomes interested in what his visitor is saying and keeps him overtime, which makes Blair, who is trying to keep things running in a tight schedule, distraught.

Stevenson usually has lunch brought in to his desk on a tray by an elderly Negro butler who has served the governors in the Mansion for years. Usually Blair and another of his aides, Carl McGowan, eat with him, talking business. Sometimes one or two of his department or division heads is also present at lunch. If more than four or five are present, or if Stevenson's sons are visiting him, or if he is entertaining some personal friend rather than business associate, he lunches upstairs in the dining room.

After lunch he continues his schedule of appointments, telephoning, and dictating till 7:00 P.M. He goes upstairs, cleans
up, and has one or two drinks, bourbon on ice. Then dinner,
frequently with business guests. Then he goes back downstairs
to his desk. He works till eleven o'clock or midnight or even
later. These, he sometimes says, are the hours when he gets his
best work done—interruptions are fewer. Then he goes to bed,
usually reading for a while first. He says he always gets eight
hours' sleep but he almost never does. Frequently he goes three
or four days without getting outside the Mansion. He is closely
prisoned by his telephone and appointment calendar. "It's a
long dreary day," Blair says.

Stevenson travels a great deal, mostly by air and mostly in
Illinois, visiting state institutions and making public appearances. He appears to enjoy these trips. He likes to get out of
the Mansion.

As an airplane passenger he is almost rash. When the weather
is too bad to fly he frequently argues with his pilot, trying to
persuade him to chance it. Once when he approached Chicago
by plane, the pilot was advised that the lake-front airport was
fogged in and they would have to land at Midway Airport.
Midway is nearly an hour's drive from the Loop and Stevenson,
reluctant to lose the time, refused to accept the radio report and
made the pilot fly to the lake front. He kept saying "Go lower
so we can see." Nobody could see anything. He said, "It doesn't
look so bad to me—let's try it." The pilot finally stood on his
prerogatives and refused and landed them at Midway. Stevenson
seemed aggrieved.

He spends less than half his time in Chicago. Blair tries to
schedule his public appearances in Chicago for Friday, Saturday,
or Sunday. Like other state officials, Stevenson is obliged to
spend a good deal of time traveling between the capital city
and the biggest city. He has an office in Chicago, on the twenty-

first and top floor of the State Building in the Loop. He is often there on Monday, having appointments at the rate of one every twenty minutes, with time out for a sandwich at his desk. He has an apartment adjoining his Chicago office and frequently sleeps there when in Chicago. This disturbs Blair—the security problem is serious. All night there is nobody in the building except the Governor and an elevator operator. Stevenson refuses to allow State Police to be posted on guard. He thinks it silly. Very recently, however, he yielded to friends' importunities and consented to having a guard posted.

Sometimes when in Chicago over a week end Stevenson spends a night at his farm in Libertyville, which is now rented by Marshall Field, Jr.

### THE MEN AROUND STEVENSON

Every Thursday morning Stevenson holds what his staff calls "skull practice"—he meets with his staff. His staff are all young men. There are six of them. They are at present Bill Blair, his appointment secretary; Bill Flanagan, his press secretary; Don Hyndman, his speech researcher; Larry Irvin, his patronage secretary; Carl McGowan, his legal adviser; and Dick Nelson, his political adviser. Frequently Ed Day, Director of the Department of Insurance, meets with them. (Day, formerly a member of Stevenson's old Sidley law firm, who married a daughter of a senior partner there, was one of Stevenson's administrative assistants until Stevenson appointed him Insurance Director.) And a former FBI man whom, as we shall see, Stevenson recently appointed to make investigations for him, also sometimes meets with the staff.

They gather about 9:00 A.M. in Blair's office and sit around, talking about the news in the morning paper or anything that comes to their minds. There is likely to be a good deal of intellectual horsing around. One April morning when I was there

they happened to be talking mostly about the presidential pref-
erence primaries then being held in various states. McGowan
was saying, "Why is Taft's showing in Wisconsin considered a
victory?" and Blair, "Because he won."

Blair, who was sitting at his desk opening the morning mail
while the others wandered around, remarked that Harold
Stassen was going to make a speech at a counrty club near
Chicago. Day asked, "Think he'll be heard above the whir of
the slot machines?"

Off to one side Hyndman and Flanagan were kidding Irvin, a
rather sober man, about being "the poor man's Pendergast,"
and Nelson was saying something about "a hell of a lot of
Republicans downstate" who liked Stevenson. McGowan began
talking about a biography of Charles Evans Hughes he'd been
reading.

There is an ebullience about them all. They wear bow ties
and crew haircuts. They like to talk and to argue. Especially
they like to deflate pomposity. They are the sort of men one
expects to find not in a politician's anteroom but in a club
patronized by young men in the arts, sciences, and professions.
The Stevenson administration has always been a rather light-
hearted reform movement.

Skull practice with Stevenson is apt to be fairly strenuous.
The subjects discussed cover the whole range of state government and politics. Sometimes somebody thinks that a state
department "is lousing things up," as a staff member puts it,
and the staff "kicks it around." Appointments to public office
are discussed. So are bills to go before the Legislature and bills
to be vetoed, public statements to be issued and positions to
be taken, public speeches to be made and public questions
to be aired. Complaints of all sorts are brought to Stevenson's
attention.

This spring a good deal of the talk has been of politics—and

of politics ranging all the way from the precinct level in Illinois
to the presidency. At one session the staff talked over the advisability of endorsing certain members of the Illinois Legislature
for renomination in the Democratic primary as well as the
advisability of Stevenson's attending various national Democratic functions in connection with Stevenson's own decision
whether or not to seek the presidential nomination.

Important policy decisions are discussed at skull practice.
Often agreement is by no means unanimous. For example, several of his advisers thought he ought not veto the Broyles loyalty
oath bill, and the matter was discussed at several meetings before
Stevenson decided to do so.

Stevenson appears to enjoy these sessions, as he enjoys any
discussion with intelligent people. He is impatient with stu-
pidity.

Once, in the fall of 1951, when Stevenson, as a potential candidate for re-election, was under heavy *Tribune* attack and
matters had become a trifle grim around the Mansion, his staff
presented him with a bulletproof vest and a pair of track shoes
together with a piece of doggerel that began:

> Up to here the Trib's only been teasin',
> But from now on it's wide-open season
> On Adlai the champ,
> So from those in your camp
> We give you these gifts with good reason.

—that is, the vest was to ward off the *Tribune*'s brickbats and
the shoes were to increase Stevenson's speed when he did run
for re-election. The doggerel also contained a couplet bespeak-
ing his staff's long-standing impatience with Stevenson's concern
about what Colonel Robert R. McCormick's *Tribune* thinks
of him:

But by the Eternal
Thumb your nose at the Colonel.

At skull practice Stevenson takes his staff into his confidence, even discussing with them such matters as rumors of a reconciliation between him and his former wife, but he never has told them what passed between him and President Truman in January when he visited Truman in Washington and reportedly received Truman's blessings on his presidential candidacy. He no doubt feels that to do so would be to violate a confidence.

His choice of men for his staff throws a good deal of light on Stevenson himself. They represent a remarkably wide range of personality and background.

William McCormick Blair, Jr., comes from a wealthy, social, and old family in Chicago. His father is an investment banker and a first cousin of Colonel Robert R. McCormick, publisher of the Chicago *Tribune*. Blair is a Republican. He attended Groton School, Leland Stanford University, the University of Virginia Law School. He is tall, slender, with dark eyes and crew haircut and a manner that some people mistake on first meeting for superciliousness. He is amusing and urbane. His somewhat flip manner conceals a deep devotion to Stevenson. His social background is similar to Stevenson's and, as has been said, he is the one that lives at the Mansion with Stevenson and travels with him more than anyone else. Blair is thirty-five.

Like Blair, Carl McGowan has an office in the Mansion across the hall from Stevenson's. Most people think that McGowan is closer to Stevenson than anyone else—that is, that Stevenson depends upon him more for advice. "McGowan is Stevenson's conscience," one man has said. "When a question involving morality comes up McGowan is always in there demanding the forthright moral position." This is a kind of advice a politician seldom receives. McGowan is a blunt plain man of forty, originally from Paris, Illinois. He attended Dartmouth and Columbia Law School. He practiced law in New York and taught law at Northwestern University. He met Stevenson while he was in the Navy in wartime Washington and Stevenson was a civilian.

McGowan said recently, smiling, "Coming to Springfield from wartime Washington was quite a shock. I'd never seen anything like this. Down there, you were interested in whether a guy was performing ably and competently. Around here if we're not careful we get to the point where we don't require ability if we can just have honesty. I never before worked in a situation where you had to be concerned about common honesty. One difficulty is of course inherent in state government. State government doesn't offer the salaries nor the scope that Federal government does. So the more intelligent people who want a government career set their eyes on Washington, not on the state capital. That has its effect all the way down the line. For example, the engineers in the highway division. Long ago they took a vow never again to stick their necks out, to mind their own damn business and use no initiative, because they'd had their heads beaten down so often. Well, you take an organization that's got its spirit licked, it's hard to revive. Stevenson went around the State and assembled the engineers and gave them a pep talk, trying to tell them this was a new deal, they dared to lift their heads and show some initiative and make themselves worth while. That's been one of the problems all along, trying to revive this state government."

Larry Irvin, Stevenson's patronage secretary, has an office in the Statehouse. He is a taciturn man of forty-one from Stevenson's own home town, Bloomington. His social background contrasts sharply with Blair's and his attitude toward public service rests on a different foundation from McGowan's. His father, a coal miner, was a Democratic precinct committeeman for fifty-two years. It is Irvin's conviction that people devotedly attached to Stevenson's political career make better state employees than Civil Service people because they don't just draw their checks and wait for 5:00 P.M. (Stevenson himself told me awhile back, "Persuaded as I am that Civil Service is the lesser of several evils, the price is very high in the way of bureaucratic rigidity. The sense of security of tenure is to one man an inspiration, to another an inducement to indifference and doing just enough to get by.") About a third of the thirty thousand state jobs under the Governor's jurisdiction are patronage jobs. Irvin, active in the Young Democrats, was to become a member of the State Democratic Central Committee this spring.

Dick Nelson is a Chicago lawyer of thirty-six who rose rapidly in politics immediately after graduating from Northwestern University Law School—he was elected president of the Young Democrat Clubs of Illinois in 1950 and a year later president of the Young Democrats of America.

Flanagan and Hyndman are former newspapermen, Flanagan from Chicago and Hyndman from downstate, both journeymen workers. Stevenson's press relations are unusually good. This is due in part to his own liking for newspapering but it is also due in great part to the skillful labors of Flanagan and Hyndman.

Thus, it has turned out that the men on Stevenson's staff today reflect remarkably well, though by chance, the eclectic sources from which Stevenson himself draws nourishment and power—wealth and social position, party politics, downstate newspapers, the law, and a moralistic approach to government.

The people wholly outside government whose advice Stevenson probably respects the most are Dutch Smith and his wife and Edison Dick and his wife.

People often have criticized Stevenson, and with reason, for being indecisive. To them he seems to postpone decisions as long as possible. To himself no doubt he postpones decisions until he has all the facts. In lawyer's terminology, Stevenson's is a judicial temperament, not an advocate's temperament. He is forever seeing all sides of a question.

Hoehler has said, "I like his open mind on everything. He never says, 'That's out.' He says, 'Very interesting.' He is a complete and thorough democrat with a small 'd.' If there's a controversy, he'll get all the interested parties to sit down and discuss it. There's a wholesomeness about him. You don't feel left out. You feel your opinion is respected. Stevenson could never be a dictator. He has too much respect for the other fellow's opinion. He has deep convictions but he also feels that others have a right to their convictions."

Stevenson listens carefully to the advice of many people. But they all say they don't know how much attention he pays to them. "In skull practice," says a staff member, "he'll listen to our advice but it's hard to tell how much of anyone's advice he takes." A final decision on major policy is rarely reached at skull practice. "He'll come to you for advice," says a close friend of his, "and when he leaves he'll say, 'Thank you so much, you've been a tremendous help to me,' and he'll apologize for burdening you with his problems. You feel it's all settled—but after he's gone you realize you don't know what he's going to do." On political matters Stevenson respects greatly the opinion of Arvey, the Cook County boss—yet in the end he makes up his own mind.

The truth seems to be that Stevenson is very much his own man.

## SCANDALS

Government is like an iceberg. The Governor or President and his cabinet are visible. But the vast bulk is submerged and hidden.

The State of Illinois employs, as has been said, some thirty thousand people under the Governor's jurisdiction. No governor can keep track of what they are up to every minute. He has to delegate his authority. History's judgment on him may depend upon how well he delegates it. For the fact that he can't do everything himself in no way relieves him of responsibility.

Government touches the life of every citizen. Its instrument may be an upright man or a thief. Governments tend to succeed or fail at the lower administrative levels. Much of Truman's trouble is there.

There is every indication that Adlai Stevenson is well aware of all this. Too well aware, perhaps. He has a New England conscience. And he is inordinately determined to succeed. Some of his aides criticize him for trying to keep track of everything, for worrying about administrative details when he ought to be making policy.

As we have seen, Stevenson replaced a governor whose administration had been scandalized several times, and he has held office during four years in which the national administration of his own party has been scandalized several times. And he has governed a state that not only has a long tradition of governmental corruption but that has a specific and extremely virulent corrupting agency at work: the Chicago Syndicate. How has Stevenson fared?

During the first two years of his administration there was no hint of scandal. The state government seemed to be running smoothly and, for Illinois, remarkably quietly. Then in the third year firecrackers began to explode.

Our purpose is not to describe in full detail the scandals of the Stevenson administration, since their details are primarily of local interest, but, rather, to indicate their nature, observe how Stevenson has dealt with them, and see what light his methods of dealing with them throws on his character.

In the fall of 1951 Chicago newspapermen, checking out information developed by the Senate Crime Committee, discovered that several legislators had been employed at Chicago Downs, a harness-racing association operating at Sportsman's Park in Cicero, after a special bill legalizing the association had passed the 1949 Legislature unanimously. The reporters checked the ownership of stock in Chicago Downs and discovered that several legislators or their wives, Chicago politicians, and state employees had been able to purchase stock for ten cents a share, stock that in a few months had yielded dividends of $1.75. And who else should turn up as a stock purchaser but Jim Mulroy, Governor Stevenson's 1948 campaign manager and since then his executive secretary, who had handled his relations with the Legislature. Mulroy had paid $100 for a thousand shares. He had got back $1,750.

Sportsman's Park, where Chicago Downs raced, has long been associated with the Capone gang and its successor, the Chicago Syndicate, not entirely because it is in Cicero. And among the other Chicago Downs stockholders listed were some names to raise eyebrows—Hugo Bennett, for example, auditor of Sportsman's, who once loaned eighty thousand dollars to a Syndicate big shot, Paul "The Waiter" Ricca; and, for another example, William H. Johnston, Jr., son of William H. Johnston, operator of Sportsman's Park and of dog tracks in Florida, of whom the Kefauver Committee report has said, "He has had a long career of close association with Chicago racketeers and the Capone gang."

The Downs stockholders' first reaction to the hue and cry was to point out that the stock was issued and bought some time after the passage of the bill, that the unanimous passage of it hardly fitted the inference that there had been a sellout, that the deal had been a "flier" of no certain outcome, that, finally, there was nothing illegal about it. (Later, a Sangamon County grand jury reached the same decision on the last point. The Illinois Harness Racing Commission also investigated, and though it discovered that some of the political purchasers had not even paid their ten cents a share until after their first dividends had come in, the Commission decided that there was no cause not to issue a 1952 license to Chicago Downs.)

That there was nothing illegal, that Mulroy had a good deal of company, that the unanimous vote in both houses made a sellout look unlikely—all this did not alter the fact that Mulroy was put in a bad light. The Chicago *Sun-Times* concluded that "if Mulroy doesn't understand [that "racetrack operators don't cut people into their profits without a reason"] he's not smart enough to be an assistant to the governor." And Clem Lane, city editor of the Chicago *Daily News,* said, "I suppose public officials will go on operating on the sordid principle that 'if it's legal, it's honest.' "

Stevenson's first reaction was to say that he thought Mulroy was guilty only of bad judgment and that he had confidence in him still. The disclosures were made in late August. On October 29 Mulroy began his letter of resignation, "I have considered most carefully, and with a full realization of your motive, our conversation of some weeks ago. There is no doubt in my mind that you believe that I would penalize myself by remaining in my present capacity." And he went on stating that to continue "might result in a definite impairment of my health" (Mulroy actually was sick; he had been hospitalized five times since March of 1948, when he was running Stevenson's campaign). Stevenson accepted the resignation with regret, agreed that Mulroy's health must come first, and concluded: "I hardly need to add to what I have often said, but let me take this occasion to again tell you of my personal appreciation for the devotion you have given your work and me."

A good deal of soul-searching preceded Mulroy's resignation.

In the interval between disclosure and resignation, public criticism of Mulroy and therefore of Stevenson had of course mounted. For weeks Stevenson had been unwilling to act. Other men in the administration had advised Mulroy to resign—he was embarrassing the Governor. Mulroy had kept saying that he'd done nothing criminal. A man who talked to Stevenson shortly after the scandal broke recalls that Stevenson was "greatly upset—he never thought Jim'd do a thing like that." Stevenson did not act for some time because of his strong feeling of loyalty to Mulroy—not only had Mulroy been one of the original Rover Boys but he had performed disagreeable and difficult service in two legislative sessions, doing a job that probably nobody else around Stevenson could have done. (Stevenson felt he owed Mulroy a great deal. It is characteristic of Stevenson that he thought more about what he owed Mulroy than about what Mulroy owed him. Mulroy died suddenly last spring and Stevenson paid his respects personally.) Today Stevenson is inclined to view the whole Chicago Downs affair calmly and even to minimize it. He says, "Jim bought the stock as a political favor. It was thoughtless, impetuous—but it wasn't dishonest. He just didn't realize what he was getting into."

The cigarette tax frauds were quite a different story. They have been termed a scandal of the Stevenson administration by Stevenson's political opponents. Stevenson himself, however, considers that the handling of them represented "a great triumph."

Somebody, probably connected with the Chicago Syndicate, stole four tax meter machines used to print state tax stamps onto packages of cigarettes. Conniving with cigarette wholesalers, they made new dies and plates and used the stolen machines to counterfeit tax stamps, thus avoiding payment of the tax. Estimates of state revenue losses ranged from three to thir-

teen million dollars. A subsequent recheck has cut the loss esti-
mate to one million.

Although crude attempts to forge cigarette tax stamps with
a hand rubber stamp had been reported from Chicago in 1947
and 1949, the first hints of a major racket came in 1951 when
Chicago cigarette dealers noticed that certain wholesalers were
cutting prices more than would be possible if they were dealing
legitimately. Fitting the facts together later, one of Stevenson's
assistants has said that the racket evidently began with the hi-
jacking of unstamped cigarettes and selling them "hot." This
racket became so big and so lucrative that it quickly outgrew its
modest strong-arm beginnings. Big shots moved in, and so, first
with the hand stamps and later with the stolen metering machines, a "business" was born.

When word that the "business" was booming reached Springfield, Stevenson instituted his own secret investigation. Ben W.
Heineman, a Chicago corporation lawyer, was named a special
Assistant Attorney General, and a private firm of investigators
was set to work. For several months they shopped in 125 retail
stores in the Chicago area, buying 361 cartons of cigarettes, 130
of which they found to be counterfeit. State police were trained
by Heineman and by Pitney Bowes, Inc., manufacturer of the
stolen tax meter machines, in the recognition of counterfeit
stamps, and on November 27, the State Police raided ten whole-
sale firms in the Chicago area. The Chicago police knew nothing
of the raids until they happened. (Just so, Stevenson had sent
State Police out to make gambling raids only after he felt that
local authorities had failed to do their own work.)

In the spring of 1952, the president of one of the raided firms
was convicted and sentenced to the penitentiary. Owners of the
other firms were awaiting trial on charges of counterfeiting
stamps, selling cigarettes bearing the counterfeits, and conspir-

ing to do both. The licenses of the raided firms were revoked, and Stevenson ordered an investigation of Department of Revenue employees, which resulted in the firing of the head of the Chicago office of the cigarette tax collection division and two inspectors who refused to take lie detector tests. A third inspector resigned.

Stevenson has said of the cigarette tax stamp "scandal": "We got on top of that one quickly and decisively."

In the backwash and uproar of the investigation that followed the assassination of a Chicago ward committeeman, Charles Gross, in February of 1952, one of Stevenson's cabinet members, Frank Annunzio, Director of Labor, found himself for the second time an embarrassment to the Governor.

A year earlier Annunzio had become the Democratic ward committeeman in the First Ward (Chicago Loop). Stevenson does not want the members of his cabinet actively engaged in politics, so he gave Annunzio his choice of his state job or his ward political job. Annunzio resigned as ward chairman.

About the same time that he became ward chairman, Annunzio formed an insurance agency with John D'Arco. D'Arco is a rising young leader of the West Side bloc in Chicago and Illinois politics, which, as we have seen, is the political action arm of the Chicago Syndicate. D'Arco had been a state legislator from a West Side ward at the time the West Side bloc helped kill Con-Con and the Crime Commission bills. D'Arco was, by 1952, alderman and Democratic First Ward committeeman.

In Anco, Inc., as the insurance agency was called, Annunzio was president, D'Arco vice-president, and another officer was a man who had been wounded in the gang killing of Hymie Weiss in the Capone days and convicted of vote fraud in 1928.

Selling insurance is one of the commonest and least dishonest methods by which Chicago ward committeemen get rich. Businessmen have to buy insurance anyway; and it is a good idea, especially in such businesses as saloonkeeping, to buy it from politicians. There are licenses, inspectors, and parking permits, and it never hurts to have an "in." Annunzio may have felt that he wanted to get into the First Ward insurance business to make sure the organization, not some individual, got the profits. He said the company was formed because businessmen kept calling him and D'Arco, asking where they could get insurance.

The Gross killing let loose the biggest series of investigations into the alliance of politics and crime that Chicago had known for twenty years, and in the process of turning over stones, Anco, Inc., came to light. Annunzio had sold his stock and resigned when he resigned his ward chairmanship. But the heat was on, and the suspicion that First Ward clout, long a force to be reckoned with in Chicago, had been reinforced by the weight of Annunzio's position in the Governor's cabinet was too much. Ten days later Annunzio resigned as Director of Labor.

Annunzio had been a CIO leader. The *Tribune* has said, with justification, that Stevenson appointed him Director of Labor to pay off a political debt to the CIO, which supported Stevenson's candidacy in 1948 (some AF of L leaders supported Green). Annunzio had not fitted in well with other men close to Stevenson. One of them, a mild man of integrity, has said sadly, "Annunzio is the kind of fellow that's always talking about 'having a piece of this and that.'" To replace Annunzio, Stevenson appointed an AF of L man who had been assistant director, and subsequently to replace him in turn, he elevated a CIO man who had been head of the conciliation service. Stevenson now points out that Annunzio had done nothing illegal. "It was a question of judgment on his part. It's just that I feel these department directors have to lean over backward."

The heaviest blow Stevenson has sustained while in office is the horsemeat scandal. In the summer of 1951 his Director of Agriculture, Roy E. Yung, reported that rumors had reached him that horsemeat was being used to adulterate hamburger. Meat is inspected by state inspectors, of course. Stevenson told Yung to investigate. Yung turned the matter over to Charles W. Wray, the superintendent of Foods and Dairies. Wray investigated and reported that nothing was amiss.

But the rumors persisted during the fall and about the end of the year investigators for the Federal Office of Price Stabilization told Stevenson they were pretty sure that horsemeat was being sold as beef by certain meat packers and that it was being done with the connivance of state inspectors. The OPS men had no definite evidence but they did have the names of several state inspectors they suspected.

Stevenson turned the matter over to his assistant, Carl McGowan, on a Thursday, January 10, 1952. Then Stevenson went to Chicago to fulfill other commitments.

At McGowan's request, Director Yung called the inspectors to Springfield. As a matter of protocol he also invited their immediate superior, Wray, the superintendent of Foods and Dairies, to attend. On Saturday morning two Assistant Attorney Generals went to the Fairgrounds in Springfield where the Agriculture Department office is located, and began questioning the inspectors. "They talked to them Saturday and Sunday," McGowan recalls. "I think they began to get uneasy right away. At four o'clock Sunday afternoon they called me and said I'd better come out, something serious was wrong."

What was wrong was that the superintendent of Foods and Dairies, Wray himself, had come under suspicion. This was almost unthinkable. Wray had been chosen for the job with great care by Stevenson himself. The reason Stevenson had used great care was that, upon taking office, he had been subjected to heavy pressure by certain politicians to appoint one of their favorites to the job. This had warned him that the crooks considered the job a lush one. He had therefore resisted all political pressure and looked long and hard for an honest man to appoint. He found Wray. Wray had been active in politics in Lake County, but he bore an impeccable reputation. He was recommended by farmers and businessmen in the foods industries alike. His family had been dubbed "typical farm family of Illinois" the year before. Stevenson was very pleased at inducing him to join the administration.

McGowan recalls, "By seven o'clock it was clear that something was wrong. The Governor was due from Chicago at eight. Then Wray said he wasn't going to say anything else until he talked to his lawyer. I told him, 'You have every right to talk to your lawyer but if you leave now, I'm going to the Mansion at eight o'clock and tell the Governor that it looks like there's something wrong, that you left town to see your lawyer—and what do you think the Governor will think?' Wray is a rather simple man greatly devoted to the Governor. He's not a racketeer. He didn't know what to do. He asked if he could telephone his lawyer. I told him, 'Sure—but the minute you pick up the telephone we'll all leave the room and you'll have crossed the line, you'll no longer be in the family.' Well, it was a very difficult thing. He paced around the room. He wept. It was most painful. Finally he told the whole story. He said he took $3,500 from Joe Siciliano, the operator of a packing plant in Lake and Henry counties, in connection with a horsemeat prosecution instituted in Lake County. Wray was approached by Siciliano and offered the money for winking at their activities."

After Wray gave his statement, Director Yung fired him. Wray was in fear of his life, not without reason, so McGowan sent him home under State Police protection and the next day turned Wray's statement over to the Lake County State's Attorney. Subsequently Wray was indicted in Lake County on charges of bribery and conspiracy. Wray has denied tae charges and repudiated what he told McGowan.

McGowan reported the whole matter to the Governor that night. McGowan recalls, "The Governor was really shocked. He put his head in his hands and said, 'My God, if Wray goes sour, I don't know, what can you depend on?' He just sat there looking at his desk. He was really quite upset."

Stevenson approved of everything McGowan had done. Further, he pressed the investigation of the inspectors under Wray. As a result at least a dozen inspectors were fired or suspended and their cases turned over to the State's Attorneys with jurisdiction.

Since then the horsemeat investigation has broadened. Horsemeat was a big racket, one involving millions of dollars. (A slush fund set up for fixes, payoffs, and other incidents amounted to $600,000). It has turned out that the Chicago Syndicate was deeply involved in the horsemeat racket. Murders have been imputed to horsemeat racketeers. In the late spring of 1952 police still were looking for an ex-convict who was fingered in a beef-hijacking and who disappeared. Police had little hope of finding him alive. They thought he knew too much about the horsemeat racket to survive. They found in his apartment a scrap of paper on which he had written "horsemeat" in Italian. He had been seen in the company of Siciliano and also in the company of Tony Accardo, usually termed the head of the Syndicate. Several local public officials have been implicated. The investigation has turned up some comment of considerable wit, as for example, Joe Siciliano's exclamation when his bond was fixed at thirty thousand dollars, "Thirty thousand! They must think I ground up Man O' War." The scandals have amused the public. Chicago gamblers, whose handbooks were closed about the same time by the Federal gambling tax, are reported to have said, "If we can't bet on 'em we might as well eat 'em." Butchers badgered housewives: "How do you want your hamburger— win, place, or show?"

Stevenson is not amused by any of this. He regards Wray's defection as a betrayal. It shook his faith in human nature. He regards it as the one failure in his administration that is inexcusable. He differentiates it sharply from the other scandals.

After the horsemeat scandal Stevenson made it clear that he did not adhere to the policy, traditional in Illinois, of permitting a public official guilty of criminal misconduct to resign but that instead he intended to see that such officials were prosecuted.

He took further steps. He appointed a former FBI man as his own investigator. Complaints that the Governor receives about state officials no longer are referred to the departments involved, which have a way of whitewashing them; they go to the ex-FBI man, who makes an independent investigation and reports direct to Stevenson. (The danger inherent in this is obvious—that a "little Gestapo" will develop. Everything depends upon the man doing the investigating and his boss.

Moreover, Stevenson, a few days after the horsemeat scandal broke, called all his department directors together in his Statehouse office and spoke to them more forcefully than ever before. He told them, in effect, "I've called you all together because I've had a bitter disappointment. Not that these inspectors were disloyal to me but that they were disloyal to themselves and to the people. Any man who seeks graft, any man guilty of corruption, is a traitor to the people. I hold myself responsible. And I hold you responsible. I want you all to know that the calm confidence I felt in the men doing their jobs is being replaced by an eager persistent surveillance on my part. I want you to understand, all of you who have people 'out in the field,' that you must have some system of accounting for how they spend their time and the things they are doing. No matter how lofty you are in your department, the responsibility for what your lowliest assistant is doing is yours." The meeting was uncomfortable.

Subsequently, the directors set up improved systems of training their inspectors and keeping track of them. Men around Stevenson have noted that, since the horsemeat scandal, he has seemed less easygoing than before and has moved faster in making administrative decisions.

People from the East sometimes ask Chicagoans if the Syndicate is anything more than "newspaper talk." It should be clear that it most certainly is. Every scandal that has afflicted the Stevenson administration has involved the Syndicate. The Syndicate is everywhere. And so are its political friends. Stevenson has not been able to keep free of them.

By studying Stevenson's handling of the scandals we can perceive two of his assets, however. He is not handicapped by the strong sense of loyalty that impels some politicians to defend their cohorts long after they have been shown to be wrongdoers, and he does not try to get off the hook by vague promises to look into matters.

### THE WEST FRANKFORT MINE DISASTER

As we have seen, one of the things that helped defeat Governor Green was the Centralia coal mine disaster. Stevenson said it wouldn't happen again if he could help it. When he took office, he procured legislation reorganizing the Department of Mines and Minerals to fix responsibility more clearly on the Director (formerly, the Director had been able to hide behind a Mining Board). He procured legislation making it a felony for a state mine inspector to accept a political campaign contribution from a mine operator, as inspectors had done under

Governor Green, and legislation increasing the number of mine rescue stations and making it easier for graduate mining engineers to become mine examiners.

Stevenson expressed satisfaction at the progress thus made. He also had an expert draw up a complete revision of the mining laws, which was badly needed. He presented this to the Mining Commission, a permanent body created years ago by the Legislature, containing representatives of the mine operators and the unions. He asked the Commission to consider this draft and to prepare a revision of the laws for submission to the Legislature. But the Commission did nothing. Surprising as it may seem to outsiders, it surprised no one in Illinois that the operators and unions alike were unwilling to work to improve mine safety. For years operators and unions have worked hand in glove to maintain the *status quo*. Stevenson next invited to breakfast all the State Senators from the mining areas and asked if one of them would introduce a bill embodying his mining law revisions. None would. One Senator did say privately he'd do it if the Governor insisted but he advised against it, since it would only antagonize the Legislature. Stevenson then told the Commission he was disappointed at the reception accorded his revision and asked the Commission to proceed with a revision of its own. The Commission did nothing. There matters stood when on December 21, 1951, an explosion in a mine at West Frankfort killed 119 men.

Stevenson's political opponents likened the disaster to the Centralia disaster. But actually they were quite different. The cause of the Centralia disaster was clear and avoidable; the cause at West Frankfort was not clear. Many warnings had been given that the Centralia mine was dangerous; the West Frankfort mine was considered a "model" mine. Centralia miners had repeatedly asked the Department of Mines and Minerals to make the company comply with the law and once had appealed to

Governor Green; no such steps had been taken at West Frankfort. Investigation after Centralia disclosed that mine inspectors had been soliciting political campaign contributions from operators; no such evidence was adduced after West Frankfort.

Governor Stevenson pointed out that until the explosion at West Frankfort, the mine safety record had been better during his administration than ever before. His opponents criticized him for not having rewritten the State's mining law. He said he had prepared a revision, he didn't know whether it would have prevented the disaster (chances are it wouldn't have), and he hadn't introduced it into the Legislature because of opposition by both operators and unions, as we have already seen. His opponents said he should have introduced it despite such opposition. He has said that to have done so would have been futile. McGowan said recently, "If Stevenson had wanted to play tongue-in-cheek politics and public relations up to the hilt, he could have introduced that bill—but he knew it wouldn't pass, so introducing it would have been an empty gesture." After the West Frankfort disaster Stevenson urged the Mining Commission to hold hearings on the causes of the disaster and the question of code revision to prevent future disasters. The Commission was somewhat reluctant to do so—an operator's man said, "In the mining fields we think the thing to do is let a thing like this settle down, not stir it up," and a union man sitting beside him concurred—and although the Commission held lengthy hearings, at which some useful evidence was adduced, particularly with reference to the need for revision of the law, to date nothing has been done.

In June of 1952, the state mine inspector at West Frankfort was fired for neglect of duty and incompetence. He told the Chicago *Tribune* that he and other inspectors had contributed one hundred dollars each to the Democratic campaign fund in the off-year, 1950, when Scott Lucas was running for re-election

to the Senate. He said he did so at the request of the Director of
the Department of Mines and Minerals, Walter Eadie, who was,
of course, a Stevenson appointee. A Stevenson spokesman replied that Stevenson had disavowed the 1950 campaign collec-
tions at that time. Eadie, before he became Director of the State
Mining Department, had been an official of the company that
owned the West Frankfort mine which blew up. It is traditional in Illinois to appoint an operator's man Director of the
State Mining Department and a union man as his assistant.
Many students of the subject have reached the conclusion that
these jobs should be held by technical experts recruited from
out-of-state mining college faculties—men not connected with
the devious coal politics of Illinois. There are some indications
that Stevenson may be contemplating making such a change.

## STEVENSON AND ALGER HISS

Some of Stevenson's opponents, notably the Chicago *Tribune*,
have criticized him for giving testimony as to the character of
Alger Hiss when Hiss was on trial in New York for perjury, a
charge that grew out of his testimony about Whittaker Chambers. Stevenson gave this testimony during Hiss's first trial. The
circumstances were these:

On May 24, 1949, the U. S. District Court in New York, before which Hiss was being tried, issued an order directing the
U. S. Commissioner in Springfield to put certain questions to
Stevenson on behalf of the Hiss defense and certain cross-ques-
tions on behalf of the prosecution. (The order was issued upon
motion of Hiss's defense attorneys. Presumably they ascertained
in advance that Stevenson would say nothing damaging to their
client, though this of course does not appear in the record.) On
June 2, the U. S. Commissioner took Stevenson's deposition at
the Mansion in Springfield.

In response to the defense questions, Stevenson said that he had known Hiss since June or July, 1933, that they had served together in the AAA legal division, that their contact then was "frequent but not close or daily," that he had no further contact with Hiss until late February or early March of 1945 when Stevenson went to work for the State Department, that he saw him then mostly at departmental meetings, that Hiss soon left for the UN conference at San Francisco and so, a little later, did Stevenson, that in San Francisco "our paths did not cross in a business way but we met occasionally at official social functions," that in July of that year in Washington Stevenson "had some conferences" with Hiss on official business, that Stevenson next saw Hiss when Hiss came to London in January of 1946, that during the first UN General Assembly there in January and February, "we had offices near-by each other and met frequently at delegation meetings and staff conferences," that he next met Hiss in 1947 during the UN General Assembly, at which time they met "on one or two occasions at my office in the United States Delegation Headquarters in connection with the budget for the United Nations." Stevenson had not seen Hiss since. He testified that he had known other persons who had known Hiss. He was asked, "From the speech of those persons, can you state what the reputation of Alger Hiss is for integrity, loyalty and veracity?" He replied that in all three respects it was good.

To the prosecution's cross-interrogatories, as lawyers call them, Stevenson responded that he never had been a guest in Hiss's home, that he had not heard before 1948 (when public charges were made) that Hiss had "removed confidential and secret documents from the State Department" and given them to unauthorized persons, that he had not before 1948 heard reports that Hiss was a Communist or a Communist sympathizer.

Everett Dirksen, in 1950 a Republican candidate for U. S. Senator from Illinois, attacked Stevenson for giving this deposition. Stevenson replied, "What would Dirksen have said?

Would he have told a lie?" The *Tribune,* which supported Dirksen, commented, "Mr. Dirksen was not a witness. The witness was Gov. Stevenson. The governor would have people believe, first, that he had no alternative but to be a witness for Hiss, and second, that he had no alternative but to give the testimony he gave. His defense is faulty on both counts . . . Gov. Stevenson cannot deny and the people of Illinois will not forget that he arrayed himself willingly beside Alger Hiss."

Last March 30 on the television program, "Meet the Press," when Stevenson's presidential boom was starting and he first underwent before a national television audience interrogation on his views on national questions, a reporter asked about his testimony in behalf of Hiss. After outlining accurately the facts as they are given above, Stevenson went on, "And I would say this—I am a lawyer, and I think that it is the duty of all citizens and particularly of lawyers, it is the most fundamental responsibility of lawyers, to give testimony in a court of law, honestly and willingly. And I think it will be a very unhappy day for Anglo-Saxon justice when a man in public life is too timid to state what he knows or has heard about a defendant in a criminal case for fear that defendant would be ultimately convicted. That is the ultimate timidity." In Chicago a group of lawyers who were watching cheered spontaneously.

## PRIVATE LIFE

On September 30, 1949, when Stevenson had been in office less than a year, he issued the following statement: "I am deeply distressed that due to the incompatibility of our lives Mrs. Stevenson feels a separation is necessary. Although I don't believe in divorce I will not contest it. We have separated with the highest mutual regard."

The explanation of the divorce usually made is that Mrs. Stevenson did not enjoy public life and resented the demands public office made on her husband's time. This, however, is not true. She says she helped her husband campaign for Governor. She preferred Springfield to Washington, where she had been with him during the war. She says she has been interested in politics for years.

The reasons for the divorce lie deeper. As long as seven years before the divorce, it had become apparent that the Stevensons' marriage had gone on the rocks. No "other woman" or "other man" is involved. Their incompatibility was a deep one and one of personalities. Mrs. Stevenson had been, as we have seen, an outstanding debutante. She was pretty, she had money, she was interested in the arts. (She still is one of the Chicago society women that ardently support *Poetry: A Magazine of Verse*.) Some of the Stevensons' friends point out that Stevenson at the time of his marriage had seemed merely a pleasant innocuous young man likely to make a small success in life, but that he became a huge success. They seem to think this explains why Mrs. Stevenson divorced him. However, as we have seen, the Stevensons were near divorce some six years before he became a great success. (The date of their first difficulty coincides approximately with his departure for wartime Washington.) Understanding such a divorce is extremely difficult, even for the two people involved. Exploring thoroughly the reasons for the Stevensons' divorce might throw some light on Stevenson's character but it would probably throw more light on his wife's character, and it would surely take us beyond the scope of this book. Mrs. Stevenson lives today in a fashionable section of Chicago, taking part in social affairs connected with the arts. She and Stevenson are on amicable terms.

The divorce hurt Stevenson deeply. He seemed crushed and lost. He told friends who knew better, "I always thought we were happily married." He felt guilty about the divorce, felt that he had failed.

Stevenson always has been fond of children. While he was living in Libertyville, his first question on coming home at the end of a day was, "Where are the boys?" He played tennis with young Adlai and taught him to shoot. His sister has said, "He neglected me for the boys."

Some of Stevenson's friends have remarked that since his divorce, he has seemed even more fond of children than before—his own and anybody else's. Friends consider that he is seeking affection now lacking in his life.

Stevenson is a lonely man. One evening awhile back when a friend of his dropped in at the Mansion, Stevenson greeted him with unusual warmth, saying, "Come on in, let's have a drink, there's nobody here, Bill Blair's away, you know, and when I'm here all alone there's nothing I can do but work." He kept his visitor until 1:00 A.M.

Sometimes his sister, Mrs. Ernest Ives, acts as his hostess. Her attitude toward him is a rather protective one. She and her husband have spent considerable time at the Mansion. She has said, "I wanted to make it seem homelike. This house here, it's a wonderful house." She remembers visiting the Mansion as a young girl. For many years it has been a tradition at the Mansion to have a large Christmas party and dance for young people. The first two Christmases of Stevenson's occupancy he maintained the tradition, with Mrs. Ives acting as hostess. The guests were his own friends and relatives and young friends of his sons. They came from Lake Forest, Bloomington, Peoria, Urbana, and other towns. Mrs. Ives recalls the occasions as joyous ones.

Stevenson's sons spent last Christmas with their mother, and Christmas at the Mansion was less gay. Moreover, the West Frankfort mine disaster had just occurred and it weighed heavily on Stevenson. On Christmas Day he entertained Mr. and Mrs. Ives, his secretary, Miss Evans, and four members of his official family and their wives and children—Carl McGowan, Ed Day, Dick Nelson, and Fred Hoehler. When the guests arrived at the Mansion about noon, they found Stevenson at work in his first-floor office. He came upstairs. They all exchanged small presents, such as neckties, and had dinner, then Stevenson went back down to his office. While he worked, Hoehler helped the children run their Christmas toys on the floor outside his office. The other guests played cards upstairs. About six Stevenson's sister persuaded him to come upstairs. He remarked, "I don't see how you people can afford to waste time playing cards." He watched for a couple of hours. About eight o'clock he picked up a newspaper and a book and, taking a glass of milk and dish of pears, went upstairs alone to bed.

Stevenson never plays cards. He plays charades very well. There is a strong streak of ham actor in him. He is often pictured as shy and retiring. Nothing could be more untrue. He likes parties, likes people, enjoys attention; he enjoys telling stories and tells them well. He drinks little. At a social gathering when a member of the party is taking motion pictures, Stevenson enjoys showing off for the camera. Every year a group of his friends from Lake Forest gives a birthday party for him, sometimes in Lake Forest, sometimes at the Mansion. At the 1950 party, when Stevenson was fifty, two of the guests enacted a little play to surprise him. One took the part of Stevenson and the other the part of William Pratt Sidley, senior partner in Stevenson's old law firm, Sidley, Austin, Burgess & Harper. The playlet contained several scenes, all brief and all nearly identical, somewhat as follows:

## SCENE I

*Time: 1933. Place: Mr. Sidley's private office. Discovered at rise: Mr. Sidley, a dignified gentleman at work. Enter Adlai Stevenson, an earnest excited young man with a high forehead.*

STEVENSON (*Breathlessly*). Mr. Sidley, Mr. Sidley, may I speak to you, Mr. Sidley, are you busy, Mr. Sidley?

SIDLEY *(Coolly).* Of course I'm busy, Adlai, but sit down.

STEVENSON. Mr. Sidley, President Roosevelt wants me to go to Washington to help with the AAA. May I go, Mr. Sidley?

SIDLEY *(Portentously).* Yes, Adlai, you may go, but I must remind you that I cannot guarantee that when you return you will be able to assume the same position you now hold in the firm or indeed that there will be a position for you of any kind.

STEVENSON. Thank you, Mr. Sidley. *(Exit at a run.)*

## SCENE II

*Time: 1934. Place: The same. Discovered: Mr. Sidley, the same. Enter Stevenson, just as eager and earnest but with a hairline that has receded a couple of inches.*

STEVENSON. Mr. Sidley, Mr. Sidley, may I speak to you, Mr. Sidley, are you busy, Mr. Sidley?

SIDLEY. Of course I'm busy, Adlai, but sit down.

STEVENSON. Mr. Sidley, President Roosevelt wants me to go to Washington to help with the Alcohol Control Administration. May I go, Mr. Sidley?

SIDLEY. Yes, Adlai, you may go, but I must remind you that I cannot guarantee that when you return you will be able to assume the same position you now hold in the firm or indeed that there will be a position for you of any kind.

STEVENSON. Thank you, Mr. Sidley. *(Exit at a run.)*

## SCENE III

*Time: 1941. Place: The same. Discovered: Mr. Sidley, the same. Enter Stevenson, every bit as eager and as earnest but with a hairline near the middle of his head.*

STEVENSON. *(Same speech.)*

SIDLEY. *(Same speech.)*

STEVENSON. Mr. Sidley, Secretary Knox wants me to go to Washington to help with the Navy, may I go, Mr. Sidley?
SIDLEY. *(Same speech.) (Same exit.)*

### SCENES IV, V, VI, VII, & VIII
*(Identical; except that the posts now in prospect for Stevenson are various ones in the State Department and the Governorship of Illinois. Also Stevenson's hairline keeps receding. Mr. Sidley is unchanged.)*

### SCENE IX
*Time: 1952. Place: The same. Discovered: The same. Enter Stevenson now looking older than Mr. Sidley, who does not seem to have aged a bit. Stevenson is now entirely bald.*
STEVENSON. Mr. Sidley, Mr. Sidley, the Democratic convention wants me to run for President, may I go, Mr. Sidley?
SIDLEY. Yes, Adlai, you may go, but I must remind you, etc.

Stevenson enjoyed the playlet hugely.

In the summer, as has been said, Stevenson likes to visit the Smiths in their summer place in Canada. "He relaxes completely up there," Smith has said. He wears shorts, a sloppy shirt, and a floppy canvas hat. He is a good canoeist. He likes to swim. He doesn't care for fishing. He likes to go on all-day canoe trips, taking a lunch. He enjoys picnics. In Canada the Smiths and other of their guests forgo a sport they favor at home, tennis. Not Stevenson—tennis is his favorite sport and he insists on playing it even in Canada, where there are many other things to do.

In 1949 the Smiths invited him to visit them there and he replied to Mrs. Smith:

Dear Ellen,

Why did you ever write me that wretched letter? Start dreaming! I shan't dream of anything else—and me with a Legislature on my hands!

You are an angel—as always—and don't be surprised if I land at the Soo some morning and call up just two hours ahead of time. And with—I hope—some boys in tow.

Affectionately,
Adlai

Stevenson delights in his farm. He likes to take his sons canoeing on the Des Plaines River near it. A few years back the farmhouse burned down and the fire destroyed many of Stevenson's family mementos. He has rebuilt the house but the mementos are of course irreplaceable.

When visiting in Lake Forest he often goes up to the next town, Lake Bluff, to play tennis with Bill Blair, whose father has an indoor tennis court on his estate. In Springfield Stevenson plays tennis at the country club and on the public courts. A couple of years ago he and Blair entered the men's doubles in the public tournament at Springfield. They lost in the first round. They are quick to point out, however, that they lost to the team that ultimately won the tournament.

Stevenson is not athletic but he would like to be considered so. If someone suggests horseback riding, or skiing, or a walk, he is quick to agree. He doesn't read much—he's too active physically. He is never still. He is always impatient. Though fifty-two, he takes steps two at a time—then tries to conceal his labored breathing.

The friends he prefers are mostly what might be called the North Shore crowd—tanned lean men in sport clothes, their well-groomed wives, people prominent in business and social circles. Stevenson, however, chooses among them rather carefully, avoiding bores and selecting people of wit and intelligence.

Since entering politics he has lost some of his old North Shore friends who could not abide an avowed Democrat. This does not disturb him—in fact, he seems to take a certain malicious pleasure in it.

Stevenson is insouciant. Awhile back when Lawrence Spivak invited him to appear on the television program, "Meet the Press," he told Spivak he had never seen the program. When in 1951 the State Senate passed his gas tax bill, Stevenson issued an official statement that began, "Hooray!"

Because Stevenson is witty and affable, because he is fun at a party, because he is an excellent toastmaster, some of his North Shore friends used to underestimate him. One of them has said, "We thought of him as a nice amusing kind of boy without realizing how much there was to him. He was the kind you always wanted to have as toastmaster. People are apt to think of that kind the same way they think of the little fat boy."

Humor is deeply ingrained in him. But there is no humor when Stevenson is discussing matters he considers of transcendent importance, such as foreign policy or race relations. Nor is there any humor when Stevenson has been beaten. In defeat, he is likely to be grim. He likes to win. A friend of his has remarked, "I don't know of anyone who'd rather win at tennis." Nor anyone who'd rather win a fight with the Legislature.

Stevenson is ordinarily of equable temperament but upon occasion he can be acerb, especially at times when he feels he is being unfairly attacked. Once he replied to Representative G. William Horsley, who had written him that stationery bearing the watermark of the Illinois State seal was being used by a Hollywood gambler in letters offering tips on horse races:

Your letter of May 2 asks for a prompt reply. You could have had a more prompt reply if you had called me by telephone but I suppose you cannot release telephone calls to the press.

The bond paper bearing the State seal watermark was purchased from the Birmingham & Prosser Company and manufactured by the Fox River Paper Company, Fox River, Wisconsin. In the manufacture of such papers there are often "over-runs." Such "ends," or "culls," are sold by the mill to the Fort Dearborn Paper Company, Chicago, a paper dealer which also sells job lot ends, rejects and imperfect papers. This company has an office in California, which probably explains how this stationery reached California.

There is nothing, I am informed, in the statutes which prohibits private sale or use of paper rejects bearing a watermark of the State seal.

I will not ask you what you mean by "these various loop holes by which the State is being milked of large sums of money each year," because you do not know yourself. But your taste for unverified accusations reminds me of the lawyer who said to the jury: "These are the conclusions on which I base my facts."

Stevenson is unorthodox. He is contemptuous of the vanities of lesser politicians. One Sunday not long after he was inaugurated he went around the state offices in Springfield, taking his picture down from the walls. He has no sycophants around him. He does not stand on ceremony. Men who have telephoned the Mansion on Saturday afternoon or Sunday have been surprised that Stevenson answers the phone himself. In a crowd he fends for himself. He travels unaccompanied by the usual retinue.

He is meticulous. In his files is a copy of his statement on Roosevelt's death, and on it he has noted in longhand that it was written mainly by Archibald MacLeish, the poet, then Assistant Secretary of State, with a phrase or two by Stevenson.

He is incisive and careful, as a lawyer should be. If a reporter asks him a vague question, he will get it cleared up carefully before answering. He is an expert at press conference fencing. He tends to control the conference without seeming to do so. He has a lawyer's analytical mind. An oil man who once saw Stevenson read and comprehend a highly technical piece of oil legislation in a few minutes said he never saw anybody master the complexities of the subject so rapidly.

Stevenson thinks fast. He is fast on his feet. Largely for this reason his appearance on the television show, "Meet the Press," was a great success. He was the most poised man on the show, though it was he who had to wrestle with the difficult questions. A person familiar with Stevenson's previous utterances and thought could see that although he had made no prior statement on many of these issues, he was able to take a position on them because he was able to fit into a framework of principles the particular facts that the questions demanded. Once, asked on another television show to name a ten-letter synonym for "security," and to do so quickly, Stevenson came up with, "For a man, employment. For a woman, engagement." (The answer wanted was "suspenders.")

A few months ago he was invited to attend a dinner in New York sponsored by the Friars Club in honor of Jack Benny's twenty-fifth anniversary in radio. Stevenson, who had assumed the dinner would be a rather modest affair, was dismayed to discover that it was being held at the Waldorf Astoria Hotel, that some two thousand people were present, and that he, though unprepared, was seated at the speakers' table. During dinner he sat between two men who seemed rather amusing. They were Fred Allen and George Burns, the comedians. Across the table was Gracie Allen, who is married to George Burns. Stevenson couldn't get it straightened out who was who. He never had heard any of these people on the radio. After dinner George Jessel, rising to serve as master of ceremonies, told

Stevenson and the other visiting dignitaries that he would call on them to say a few words and then would call on the professional entertainers, such as Fred Allen and George Burns, so the politicians wouldn't have to follow the pros. Stevenson took comfort in observing that none of the others near him had a prepared text.

Jessel, however, abandoned his announced intention. He called on the other politicians but not on Stevenson. After the other politicians had spoken, Jessel called on Fred Allen. Allen unfolded his menu and inside it Stevenson saw a complete speech text, with words carefully capitalized and underlined in red for emphasis. Allen delivered it, and the applause was tumultuous. When Allen sat down, Jessel called on Stevenson. Stevenson has since said, "I was never so absolutely terrified in my life."

He arose. Some in the audience still were tittering at memory of Allen's hilarity. Stevenson has said, "I did the only thing I could think of. I said, 'Ladies and gentlemen, during the course of the dinner Mr. Allen and I were discussing what we would say here tonight. We traded manuscripts so that each of us could take a look at the other's speech. You have just heard Mr. Allen deliver my speech. And I must say he delivered it very well. As for Mr. Allen's speech, I have it here but I don't think it would amuse you.' " He brought down the house.

In his personal relationships, Stevenson is a warm friendly man. When his Libertyville neighbor and friend, Lloyd Lewis, the author, died, Stevenson attended the funeral. He was called on unexpectedly to say a few words. He said: "I have been asked to share in these farewells to a friend.

"I think it is a good day for this meeting. It is April now and all life is being renewed on the bank of this river that he loved so well. I think we will all be happy that it happened on this day, here by the river with the spring sky so clear, and the west wind so warm and fresh. I think we will all be the better for this day and this meeting together.

"He was my neighbor. He was the neighbor of many of you. He was a very good neighbor; quick in time of misfortune, always present in times of mirth and happiness—and need.

"I think Mr. [Marc] Connelly [the playwright] was right when he said he was the most successful man he ever knew. I don't know much about the riches of life, and I suspect few of you have found the last definition. But I do know that friendship is the greatest enrichment that I have found.

"Everyone loved this man. He enriched others and was enriched. Everyone was his friend—everyone who knew him or read him. Why was that? Why is he the most successful man that many of us will ever know? Our answers will differ. For me it was his humility, gentleness, wisdom and wit, all in one. And most of all a great compassionate friendliness.

"I think it will always be April in our memory of him. It will always be a bright, fresh day, full of the infinite variety and the promise of new life. Perhaps nothing has gone at all—perhaps only the *embodiment* of the thing—tender, precious to all of us—a friendship that is immortal and doesn't pass along. It will be renewed for me, much as I know it will for all of you, each spring."

Stevenson is frugal as only the rich can afford to be. Touring in the 1948 campaign he left only his customary fifteen per cent tip for waitresses; Kohn or one of his other advisers would leave the dollar bill expected of candidates. He used to go around the Mansion turning off lights to save on the electric bill. He worried about the heating bill. He has cut down greatly the governor's entertaining budget, especially the portion of it that went for liquor. Campaigning, he wore an old Brooks Brothers hat despite the entreaties of Mulroy and Kohn that he get a new one and one with a wider brim. Once Mulroy tried to throw the old one away but Stevenson retrieved it and admonished Mulroy that wastefulness was wicked.

Like many men of means, Stevenson is extremely reticent about his private finances. His salary as Governor is $12,000 a year. His private income has been estimated at about $50,000, mostly from the *Pantagraph,* and his net worth at about $500,-000. Stevenson will neither confirm nor deny the figures. A friend thinks they may be a little high. He has said, "Adlai is always worried about money. Especially since he's been Governor. He complains that he's been obliged to go into his capital." It has been estimated that it costs a man about $50,000 a year to be Governor of Illinois.

There are several cornerstones to Stevenson's character. One is his aloneness (which some people take to be part of his reserve and mistake for aloofness). His loneliness is clearly evident in his personal life but it also is evident in his official acts: as has been said, he makes his own decisions, he is his own man.

Another is his very deep sense of security. He is calm, confident, and he does not have to strive to appear so; he is deeply secure. Money and family produce this kind of security. So does a tranquil, loving atmosphere in one's childhood home. So do the right schools, right not only in the social sense but in the intellectual sense: Choate Preparatory School is socially "correct" and it also gives a boy the Latin classics that, if used, can provide him with firm ground to stand on. Stevenson makes use of things like that. He never has experienced a corrosive feeling that most people know: envy. He is one of the fortunate few who has been able to feel always that there's nothing better than what he possesses. (It is this deep security, coupled with an innate humility, that puzzles some people. They say, "He's a paradox—he's shy but confident.") This same feeling of security underlies his belief in the inviolability of the individual. His respect for the individual is more than a political idea; it is a personal article of faith.

Another cornerstone of his character is that he is a moral creature. He is more concerned with the rightness or wrongness of a matter than with its legality.

Stevenson is an integrated man. His character, his intellectual judgments, and his official acts are all of a piece. He is an active thinker. He does not think in a vacuum—he relates. Relates his administrative policies tightly to his own personal faith. For example, from his belief in the importance of the individual comes his opinion that the fundamental strength of American democracy rests on the assumption of local responsibility; and from that come his views on a variety of issues, such as his view on a Federal Fair Employment Practices Commission. He has said that he believes states should regulate their own affairs insofar as they do so well, that he would hope the problem of civil rights could be solved by the states, that he has fought in two legislative sessions for an Illinois FEPC, that if ultimately the states fail to safeguard civil rights then the Federal Government must, for in the long run all citizens must be guaranteed equality of opportunity without regard to their race, creed, or color. And many of his administrative policies come from his determination that local authorities shall perform local functions whenever possible. Only with reluctance did he send his State Police out on gambling raids, and he has sought to procure more and more community participation in the State Welfare Department's programs.

All this is to say that Stevenson meets new issues not piecemeal, one by one, as does an opportunist; he attacks them from positions thought out long in advance, positions that come from his deepest beliefs. (This makes it hard to compare him with other persons. He has been compared with Roosevelt, for example. But Roosevelt was an innovator, and Stevenson is not;

he is in a stricter sense a reformer—he is inclined to repair and tighten up and improve existing structures. And Roosevelt was an improviser, making up a program as he went along, with no apparent foundation in theory or belief, while Stevenson gives the impression always of acting on principle. And where Roosevelt led firmly—some said dictatorially—Stevenson guides.) Fred Hoehler has said, "He leads by inspiration. He inspires the rest of us to do things. It works among the people at large too— the strength of his conviction on FEPC would persuade others." More than one person meeting Stevenson for the first time has come away inspired to work in his administration or for his election. More than one has caught fire from him.

Stevenson's habit of thinking things through hardheadedly for himself is at once his greatest weakness and his greatest strength. It is the quality that makes people call him indecisive. And it is the quality that makes him seem new and original. He uses all his eclectic education which encompasses, as we have seen, newspapering, farming, the law, politics, prominent family, Lake Forest, a classical schooling. This is why his decisions sometimes surprise. He is hard to pigeonhole. It is impossible to call him a "liberal" or a "conservative." He makes a shifty target for a political opponent. Ordinary labels do not fit him.

Stevenson could be called a gradualist. He moves slowly, not in spectacular rushes. He is also a practical man. When he set about the task of taking the State Police out of politics, he didn't do so all at once—he procured a law providing that temporarily half of the police should be Republicans and half Democrats. Subsequently all the police were put on a merit basis. An academic expert in public administration criticized him for not going all out for Civil Service immediately. Stevenson considered this dreamy.

Stevenson works very hard at the job of being Governor. If you ask him about his private life these days he is likely to reply, "I haven't any." Few Americans realize how great are the demands they make upon the time of their high public officials. Stevenson's schedule is, as we have seen, extremely heavy. Stevenson once was moved to reflect publicly upon the business of being Governor. Less than a year after he was elected he told the Chamber of Commerce at Litchfield, Illinois: "You know, before I somewhat unexpectedly became a politician I used to be just a simple, barefoot LaSalle Street lawyer, a farmer, and a sort of intermittent—itinerant—government servant and diplomat. I used to lecture occasionally at universities and before audiences around the country on foreign affairs. They even paid me fees to talk—which is another reason politics is not as attractive as it should be. It was a cinch. In those days after the war all you had to do was to talk darkly about the atomic bomb, bacteriological extermination, the decline and fall of the British Empire, damn the sinister Russians, beat your breast self-righteously about the United States and wind up with a fervent prayer for the United Nations, and a five- or six-point program; five or six points depending on whether you thought you could get away with a demand for tax reduction, economy and more free enterprise, coupled with emphatic insistence on an impregnable national defense in the atomic age and a plea for America financing a world crusade to stop Communism. It may sound hard to you, but it's a cinch; you can't miss! The audience approves of everything you say. They're spellbound. When you've finished they thank you nervously and earnestly for your message—what a word!—and wander into the night with their apprehensions confirmed, their confusion enlarged and their perspective diminished. Well, that's all changed now—my horizons are the State of Illinois.

"When I decided to run for Governor last year I did so with my eyes wide open; I knew it was a job involving many problems and many responsibilities. It didn't take me long to find out I wasn't wrong—I had merely underestimated. I found that the problems that are laid on the Governor's doorstep from day to day are of infinitely greater variety than the average citizen realizes. It is an office in which there has been a tremendous growth of responsibility in the last two decades or so. It is one of those jobs in which there are no hours and no holidays; in which you literally work day and night, and pause every once in a while to wonder if you are really getting any place in accomplishing the things you are trying to do.

"In one respect at least, it reminds me of international conferences and something I wrote in London in a weary moment:

> I live in a sea of words
> Where the nouns and the adjectives flow;
> Where the verbs speak of actions
> That never take place
> And the sentences come and go.

"I found too that in many respects the governorship is a paradox. Because it is the highest elective office in the State, people are inclined to think that the Governor can do anything or everything. Actually, the Governor's authority is very definitely limited by the constitution and by our statutes. But a great many people seem to have the idea that all I have to do is snap my fingers and magical things will happen; that a bridge will be built, a new highway will go in, or even that I can get your Federal income taxes or your rent reduced—or that an airport will appear. I am happy to say, by the way, that we hope to be of some help to your Litchfield airport.

"Frankly, I have been surprised and a little startled by the faith which many people, who are not very familiar with the processes of our government, have in the power of the Governor. Some of the appeals that are made to me through the mails are amazing. Just this week a woman wrote me a letter suggesting I compel her ex-husband to pay her twelve hundred dollars back alimony. A man wrote to ask whether I thought it was true that Sam Houston once shot an Indian at five thousand yards, and shooting over a hill at that! Various people who write songs send their efforts to me for judgment and endorsement, even though I can't carry a tune. And I was cautioned at an early age to diminish my volume in church.

"A mysterious note came to my desk the other day. It was very brief: 'Look into License No. So and So, 1948 Black Ford Sedan.' The note was signed 'Conscientious Objector.' A farm wife wrote demanding that I do something to keep her neighbors' cattle, whose pedigree she judged to be much lower than that of her own herd, from mingling with her livestock and thus endangering the breed. Even the young credit me with vast powers. A fifth-grade farm boy wrote to ask whether he could be compelled to 'walk further than my mailbox' to catch the school bus. I suspect he was looking to me for an excuse to get out of going to school. Having ridden a bicycle four or five blocks myself I couldn't write him an exemplary letter about how I trudged three miles through snow and ice morning and evening to win a little education.

"Dozens of other examples could be cited, but that gives you an idea. About five hundred people write to me every day, on the average. At times, as during legislative sessions, when people were making known their views on pending bills, the volume of correspondence was much greater.

"A considerable part of the Governor's mail consists of invitations to attend various public functions. If I were twins I couldn't accept one-tenth of these invitations and get any work done. In fact, I cannot accept as many as I would like to, and still do justice to my responsibilities to the state government, which is the biggest business in the State. Invitations of one kind or another for public appearances average eight or ten daily, and I am not sure whether I should be flattered or whether it's merely a case of people being curious to see what I look like.

"But I do like my job, and I am grateful to those of you in Litchfield and Montgomery County who helped put me in office. At the same time I think I understand why defeated candidates always congratulate victors. I not only like my job, I want more than I have ever wanted anything to improve the quality of public administration in Illinois."

# CHAPTER VI

# Stevenson and the Presidency

GOVERNOR ADLAI STEVENSON, the man who put Illinois government into a button-down collar, is a relatively low-pressure individual. After President Truman renounced renomination on March 30, 1952, large numbers of prominent Democratic politicians, private citizens, and uplifters besought Stevenson to announce his own candidacy. His long-distance phones were jammed day after day, his mail piled up hopelessly, so many newspapermen and magazine writers descended on the Mansion at Springfield that it was manifestly impossible for him to spend much time with them all and they were reduced to interviewing each other.

Through it all, Stevenson, sitting at his desk as usual in a pair of rumpled slacks and a corduroy jacket or a Princeton jacket, seemed unperturbed. The Mansion, which one might have expected to become bedlam, lost none of its quiet charm. Blair and the Governor's aides fooled around as usual before the weekly skull practice, Carol Evans spent some little time assuring a neighbor down the street that she needn't be concerned about a visit paid her by the Governor's dog—"He's always wandering away, he'll come home"—and on April 1 somebody pasted a piece of paper lettered "April Fool" across the mouthpiece of a telephone in the Governor's office.

It is pleasant to report that the Rover Boys are not shriveled with age. Nor have they slicked up their operation—liaison among them was almost as poor as during the 1948 campaign, and an experienced newspaper reporter, Ed Lahey, was pleased to observe that matters were a great deal more confused than at Albany in 1948, when Governor Dewey was winding up his mechanical engine.

When 1952 began, Stevenson was almost unknown outside Illinois to the populace at large. By late spring he had become a national figure. This had come about in a curiously left-handed way. It had resulted from his repeated declaration that he didn't want to run for President in 1952. While other candidates were huffing and puffing about the country posing in bizarre costume for cameramen and by other means trying to attract attention, Stevenson just kept saying he didn't want to run. The response was a yawn for the others and bale after bale of publicity for him. Because a similar technique is commonly employed in romance—playing hard to get—people assumed that Stevenson was being coy. The curious thing is that he wasn't. He just didn't want to run for President in 1952.

He told me this early in February of 1952. (He had been telling others the same thing almost from the first day he took office at Springfield, in 1949, though at that time their talk was a good deal more idle than it was by 1952.) In March of 1952, shortly before Truman took himself out of the race, Stevenson told me, "People don't believe me, but I'm absolutely frank when I say I don't want to run for President. And having said that I'll be equally frank and say that four years from now, that's another matter. If by then it has become clear that I'm going to be a politician all the rest of my life—I'll be too old to do anything else anyway—and if by then I have the sense of self-confidence it takes and I've had a chance to get this Illinois business done, why then yes, I might want to be a candidate. My boys will be grown up by then too.

"For right now, I think the thing to do is to stay in Illinois and finish the job. I've only got started. Well started. But I want four more years at the job. I feel a sense of obligation to finish the job. You just don't run out on a job like that, by God. It's like accepting an invitation to dinner and then you get a better invitation and you cancel the first one. You just don't do that kind of thing. It isn't cricket."

I am convinced that Stevenson's reluctance to run in 1952 was genuine. He did not want to for a number of reasons.

First of all he honestly wanted to stay on in Illinois and finish the job he started. He feared that a successor would scrap many of the programs he set in motion. Furthermore, he felt a deep obligation to the public-spirited men whom he persuaded to join his administration. He didn't want to run out on them.

Second, he probably did not want to run against Eisenhower. As we have seen, Stevenson likes to win. In the early spring of 1952 Eisenhower looked hard to beat. Not only that, but Stevenson could not make his strongest campaign against Eisenhower, since they were close to agreement on foreign policy.

Third, Stevenson had personal or family reasons for not wanting to run this year. He feared that the glare of publicity at the White House might be harmful to his sons. Four years from now they would be four years older. (The youngest is now sixteen.) Moreover, Stevenson is a lonely man and the White House is probably the loneliest house in the world. Stevenson would be one of the loneliest presidents since Lincoln.

Fourth, Stevenson may have felt, though he never would say it publicly, that the Democratic bureaucrats have become so deeply entrenched in Washington during the past twenty years that no Democratic President taking office now could rule well.

A thorough bloodletting, which only a Republican President could perform, might pave the way for a Democrat to start afresh four years hence. Moreover Stevenson felt, I believe, that the American public has become so distracted by criticisms of the Truman administration that it has lost perspective on the problems facing the nation. Stevenson told me, "The public has got to realize that the issues facing this country are bigger than a mink coat or an intemperate letter. And these monstrous problems can't be solved by imputations and charges of Communists in the government." Stevenson doubted that Eisenhower could solve the country's difficult problems with the kind of Republican leadership he'd have in the Senate. But, Stevenson may have felt, four years of Republican rule might clear the air and focus attention on the issues.

During March and April, Stevenson's admirers pressed him to declare himself a presidential candidate. He kept silent. They continued to press him, saying that time was short. Finally on April 16, Stevenson, under great pressure for a statement of some sort, issued this one:

I have been urged to announce my candidacy for the Democratic nomination for President, but I am a candidate for Governor of Illinois and I cannot run for two offices at the same time. Moreover, my duties as Governor do not presently afford the time to campaign for the nomination even if I wanted it.

Others have asked me merely to say that I would accept a nomination which I did not seek. To state my position now on a prospect so remote in time and probability seems to me a little presumptuous. But I would rather presume than embarrass or mislead.

In these somber years the hopes of mankind dwell with the President of the United States. From such dread responsibility one does not shrink in fear, self-interest or humility. But great political parties, like great nations, have no indispensable man, and last January, before I was ever considered for the presidency, I announced that I would seek re-election as Governor of Illinois. Last week I was nominated in the Democratic primary. It is the highest office within the gift of the citizens of Illinois, and its power for good or ill over their lives is correspondingly great. No one should lightly aspire to it or lightly abandon the quest once begun.

Hence, I have repeatedly said that I was a candidate for Governor of Illinois and had no other ambition. To this I must now add that in view of my prior commitment to run for Governor and my desire and the desire of many who have given me their help and confidence in our unfinished work in Illinois, I could not accept the nomination for any other office this summer.

Better state government is the only sound foundation for our Federal system, and I am proud and content to stand on my commitment to ask the people of Illinois to allow me to continue for another four years in my present post.

I cannot hope that my situation will be universally understood or my conclusions unanimously approved.

I can hope that friends with larger ambitions for me will not think ill of me. They have paid me the greatest compliment within their gift, and they have my utmost gratitude.

This was not a statement like Sherman's telegram to the Republican convention in 1884: "I WILL NOT ACCEPT IF NOMINATED, AND WILL NOT SERVE IF ELECTED." Stevenson probably is incapable of such a statement. His statement of April 16 is about as close as he could come to taking himself out of contention.

But a curious thing happened. His statement was greeted with a few remarks, such as that of Arvey, the Cook County boss, who said, "I can't see how any patriotic Democrat could turn down a draft." And then ensued a great silence, lasting some six weeks. During this period various other Democratic candidates appeared. None caught fire. (Nor, for that matter, did Eisenhower at Abilene.) By the middle of June the papers were again full of speculations on Stevenson's intentions. And

Springfield was once more full of visiting reporters and Democratic convention delegates. Curiously Stevenson in 1952 occupied almost precisely the same position as in 1948—that of being urged to run for an office he didn't want. The draft was not manipulated. Stevenson himself did nothing to arrange it. (In fact, he did worse than nothing: he kept urging people not to try to nominate him, as when he announced that he wished he could have his name removed from the primary ballot in Oregon.) Nor did the party leaders maneuver in secret. Colonel Arvey said he hadn't spent three cents for a stamp or ten cents for a phone call yet he was besieged by political leaders eager to throw their convention delegates to Stevenson. "I never saw anything like it," Arvey said.

What had happened? Obviously, something extraordinary: a spontaneous draft.

The reasons are not hard to find. The American presidency is the depository of enormous power. When it is suddenly vacated—as Truman did vacate it—a vacuum results, a tremendous power vacuum. Somebody *must* fill it. No other Democrat who announced his willingness to do so looked able to do so.

For the Democrats had problems, and underlying their problems were the nation's. Stevenson rose so swiftly to national prominence because of the internal difficulties of the Democratic Party and the nation and because of the independence of Stevenson's mind and record.

For fourteen years, as Samuel Lubell has pointed out in his recent book, *The Future of American Politics,* the Democratic Party has been paralyzed by internal conflicts. These conflicts are the symptoms of a political revolution that has taken place in America in the last twenty years. The issues raised by the revolution have been fought out inside the Democratic Party, not inside the Republican Party. The result has been that at every convention, from the third-term convention of 1940 onward, the Democratic coalition patched together by Roosevelt has been in danger of flying apart.

In 1952, when Truman renounced renomination, acute politicians said at once that Adlai Stevenson looked like "the only man." They meant that he is the only man who can hold together the Democratic coalition—the Southern Dixiecrats, the Northern Negroes, and the big-city bosses, the "labor-liberal" voters, and the farmers.

Taking them in order, Stevenson is acceptable to Governor James Byrnes of South Carolina and Senator Richard B. Russell of Georgia. ("Hell," says a politician, "he's a cousin of Russell's.") Moreover, he is a states' rights man.

His record on civil rights and equality of opportunity is unimpeachable; he fought for FEPC in two Illinois Legislatures.

He understands and does not shun the biggest big-city machine of them all, Arvey's Cook County machine.

He picked up labor-liberal support before World War II by his opposition to isolationism; he has held it since by such measures as calling a special session of the Legislature to get rent control for municipalities, defending civil rights, vetoing the Broyles loyalty oath bills, and above all by his reform administration.

He holds farm support on his record and background, which extends back to AAA and beyond.

But above all and more important than his ability to hold together the Democratic coalition, Adlai Stevenson in the spring of 1952 looked like the only man in sight capable of giving the Democratic Party a new direction for the first time since 1932. In those twenty years since Roosevelt first was nominated, a whole new generation of voters (and of party workers and bureaucrats) has grown up. A prewar depression has passed and so has a war. The American economy, the American foreign policy, the American social order, and the role of government in America, have been revolutionized in those twenty years. But both political parties, because of a continuity of leadership, have tended to meet new problems with old solutions that do not always fit. It is absurd that the Democrats still campaign against the Hoover depression, that the Republicans campaign against "that man" in the White House. Time and events have outdistanced the politicians. They know they need new blood. This may explain Eisenhower's rise in the Republican Party. And now for the first time in the Democratic Party too the continuity of leadership has ended. Truman has stepped down. The link with the past is broken. An opportunity has arisen for the Party to take new direction. And Stevenson, because he would bring to the new conditions of America an independent mind and a politics not bound by the past, looked like the best man available to lead it.

The draft of Stevenson, a phenomenon of the utmost importance, did not really occur during the convention. It took place during the spring. When Truman withdrew, several politicians rushed in to try to fill the void, mistaking the nature of the void. They thought it was primarily a political void and therefore could be filled by any politician agile enough. They were wrong. More had happened than that the party had lost its leader.

The draft of Stevenson evolved through three stages, and they all three were alike. During the first phase, from February to June, Stevenson was reluctant to run, the other candidates made their canvasses, none succeeded. During the second phase, in July just before the convention, Stevenson was still reluctant, the other candidates arrived in Chicago, and the more they talked the more apparent it became that no single one was completely suitable. Finally, during the convention balloting,

Stevenson had become unwillingly resigned to accepting the nomination, the other candidates each in turn made their bids, all failed, and Stevenson was nominated.

That convention may have puzzled people. Some of the people close to Stevenson were disappointed that he was not nominated on the first ballot. They feared that a nomination on a later ballot would not be a "genuine draft" but a connived nomination. But they were confusing a convention with a popularity contest. A convention is a convocation of diverse and often conflicting forces. When so large a void is created as was created by Truman's withdrawal, all the variegated parts of the apparatus that fills it must be rearranged before they will fit into it. American political parties are—must be—coalitions which represent the diverse and conflicting needs of a large and polyglot population. (This is why a true left-right split never has occurred in this country.) If Stevenson was to be nominated it had to be by all of his party except a few irreconcilables. It follows that deals had to be made. But the deals were not made for him; they were made in the process of rearranging the party around him. Indeed, the very fact that he was not nominated on the first ballot demonstrates the magnitude of the upheaval that brought Stevenson to the top. A one-ballot convention would have meant that the party remained the same. The 1952 Democratic convention means that the party has been broken to pieces and that the pieces have rearranged themselves. The draft of Stevenson was, I believe, the product of historical necessity. This is why Stevenson could not succeed in saying no. It is why the party swallowed its pride and took him after he had rebuffed it. Both Stevenson and the party were caught in a major historical shift. It is true of course that just as politicians are always abusing the word "draft" so are they also every four years proclaiming a "new era." Nevertheless, I think it not unlikely that historians will consider 1952 a decisive turning point in America's course, comparable, say, to 1860 or 1932.

### A WALK AROUND THE BLOCK

About nine o'clock one April morning I was waiting for Stevenson in the quiet anteroom of his Chicago office when he came out of his private office and asked if I wanted to go have coffee with him. He was wearing an oxford-gray flannel suit. He looked, as usual, freshly shaved. He had spent the night in his office—"my cell," he calls it.

We rode down twenty-two floors in the elevator. At the bottom Stevenson waited for two girls who worked for the State to leave the elevator first, smiling at them and motioning for them to precede him when they hesitated. We went into the drugstore in the State Building. Stevenson ignored the booths and stepped up to the counter. He said, "Looks like there's no two vacants together." A man alone turned to eye him sourly, recognized him, started, and said, "Here, Governor," and moved over.

Stevenson ordered bacon and eggs and toast and coffee, and ate while I was drinking a cup of coffee, then asked if I minded walking around the block once.

As we started I asked if he did it often. He said, "No, I don't get a chance to do anything worth while anymore." I remarked about his walking in Chicago's Loop without a guard. He seemed surprised—it hadn't occurred to him. He laughed. "Bill Blair's always worried about what he calls the security problem," he said. "Always after me to have a State Policeman down here at the building. I think it's silly—why anyone should want to come up twenty-two floors to do anything to me is beyond my comprehension."

A man on the street stopped him. Stevenson shook hands and talked to him a moment. Walking on, he said to me, "A West Side legislator, very decent sort, too." Several other people recognized him. He appeared not to notice. He was walking fast and breathing deeply and talking about the exercise he used to get. He seemed to be enjoying the walk.

Back in his office, a large bright clean-looking room overlooking the Loop, I asked him what he considered his greatest accomplishment and his greatest failure as a governor. He pulled a pad of lawyer's yellow paper over and picked up a sharp pencil and made some notes as he talked, as though clarifying his thought. It wasn't necessary—the most important thing to him came to his mind first: "The men I've brought into government. Then, a change in the tone and pace in state government. Then aid to the schools—it's a little hard." He put down his pencil. "As far as the legislative program is concerned, the schools. As for administration, the men I've brought in. The men—that's the most important. We've lifted government up out of the sort of dead cynical level in which it'd been mired for so long and got people working with some enthusiasm. Government is a series of delegations. Unless you delegate well, delegate to competent, scrupulous, and vigorous men, you fail.

"Now, as to failures—it's the same thing. The element of human failure. It's a constant heartbreak, this evidence of disloyalty and this infinite difficulty you confront in trying to get scrupulous people into every position." He talked about some failures in his legislative program—Con-Con ("But there we got the Gateway Amendment so we didn't lose everything"), FEPC ("There again we came within an ace and we pressed them so hard that I think we persuaded private business to clean up its own house"), liquor and gambling bills ("It was the first time they'd ever been tried"). "No, some of our legislation didn't succeed but on the whole we received a dividend in nearly every case. The worst thing, the most disheartening thing, is having a man go wrong on you. Of course, I suppose it's inevitable that there would be some failures. After all, we are trying to end something that's been common practice for one hundred years. But at least we've started."

Once, while gathering material on Stevenson, I told a friend of his at the end of one interview that I was afraid I'd have to see him again. He said, "That's all right—I already have so much time and enthusiasm invested in Adlai that a little more doesn't bother me." A lot of people feel that way.

# Acknowledgments

For help in the preparation of this book I owe a large debt to Louis A. Kohn and Francis S. Nipp. Kohn, a Chicago lawyer who was one of Stevenson's earliest backers in 1947, gave me free access to his files and furnished great quantities of material. Nipp, a lecturer in English at Roosevelt College and long a personal friend of mine, did the preliminary spadework on the Governor's papers and then performed research and editorial labor. My wife, Frances Smethurst Martin, helped by encouraging the preparation of the book and typing the manuscript. For help in obtaining material I owe thanks to Governor Stevenson's administrative aides, especially William McCormick Blair, Jr., Carl McGowan, T. Don Hyndman, and William I. Flanagan; to Stevenson's secretaries, Carol Evans, Margaret Munn and Phyllis Gustafson; to Flanagan's assistants, especially Mary Watt and Merle Wood; to Mr. and Mrs. Hermon Dunlap Smith of Lake Forest; to Fred K. Hoehler, Director of the Department of Public Welfare; to Stevenson's former wife, Mrs. Ellen Borden Stevenson; and of course to Governor Stevenson himself. The responsibility for the use of the material they furnished is, of course, mine alone.